DATE DUE 5 22 12

9 13 11

101 Tips
for
Running a
Successful
Home
Business

Proven Strategies and Sage Advice
for the At-Home Entrepreneur

D0283463

101 Tips
for
Running a
Successful
Home
Business

Proven Strategies and Sage Advice
for the At-Home Entrepreneur

MAXYE AND LOU HENRY

Phillipsburg Free Public Library

LOWELL HOUSE
LOS ANGELES

NTC/Contemporary Publishing Group

f Congress Cataloging-in-Publication Data

xye.
    101 tips for running a successful home business: proven strategies and sage
advice for the at-home entrepreneur / Maxye & Lou Henry.
        p. cm.
    Includes bibliographical references and index.
    ISBN 0-7373-0421-9 (alk. paper)
    1. Home-based businesses—Management. 2. New business enterprises—
Management.
    I. Title: One hundred one tips for running a successful home business. II. Henry,
Lou, 1944- III. Title.

    HD62.38 .H455 2000
    658'.041—dc21   00-032329

Excerpt from *Feng Shui at Work*, by Kirsten M. Lagatree, copyright 1998, reprinted with
permission of Villard Books.

Excerpt from *The Perfect Business*, by Michael LeBoeuf, copyright 1996 by Michael LeBoeuf,
Ph.D., reprinted with permission of Simon & Shuster and Author Pine Associates, Inc.

Published by Lowell House
A division of NTC/Contemporary Publishing Group, Inc.
4255 West Touhy Avenue, Lincolnwood (Chicago), Illinois 60712-1975 U.S.A.

Lowell House books can be purchased at special discounts when ordered in bulk
for premiums and special sales. Contact Department CS at the following address:
NTC/Contemporary Publishing Group
4255 West Touhy Avenue
Lincolnwood, IL 60712-1975
1-800-323-4900

Roxbury Park is a division of NTC/Contemporary Publishing Group, Inc.

Managing Director and Publisher: Jack Artenstein
Editor in Chief, Roxbury Park Books: Michael Artenstein
Director of Publishing Services: Rena Copperman
Editor: Rachel Livsey
Editorial Assistant: Nicole Monastirsky
Interior Designer: Anna Christian

Printed and bound in the United States of America
00 01 02 DHD 10 9 8 7 6 5 4 3 2 1

To Irving and Esther Spens
and
Louis and Claudia Henry,
who always encouraged us to do our best,
no matter what careers we chose.

Contents

Acknowledgments

*Many thanks to the home-based businesspeople
who shared their experiences
so that this book could be written.*

Introduction

This book is for those of you who have already established your home-based business. To help your enterprise thrive and grow, we have gathered 101 tips that will enable you to focus your efforts, cope with many of the problems that home-based businesspeople face every day, and move forward toward the rewards and success you have set out to achieve.

Many solo entrepreneurs launch service-centered businesses with a minimal investment—perhaps just a computer and a telephone in a convenient corner. Others start businesses out of their workshops and artists' studios. Our tips on office design and equipment will show you how to make any workspace more efficient. Other suggestions describe how home businesses can take advantage of off-site facilities when necessary, to compete with conventional businesses that have invested in commercial real estate and staffing. We offer lots of ideas for those who operate businesses such as bed-and-breakfast inns or in-home day-care facilities, where family activities may be an integral part of the business.

These tips are designed for a home business that's gotten off to a running start and now needs an infusion of fresh ideas in order to sustain that momentum for greater efficiency and profit. Being a solo entrepreneur or a partner in a home-based business isn't easy, and requires wearing many hats. We'll show you how to decide whether to tackle a particular task yourself or outsource that chore to someone else. Our marketing ideas will help you evaluate customer satisfaction, keep current customers, encourage repeat business, and attract new clients.

Tips from successful home workers describe ways for solo entrepreneurs to maximize their skills and stay motivated, even when distractions beckon, procrastination immobilizes, or isolation threatens to make them feel out of touch with the world.

Every year, more and more people recognize the advantages of working from home and choose this lifestyle. As this trend continues into the future, new products and technology will be required to serve the needs of the home workplace. Those of us who are already experienced at "minding our home business" are in an excellent position to develop innovations for the next generation of home workers.

Read on, with our best wishes for your continued success!

—*MAXYE AND LOU HENRY*

How to Use This Book

You can read these tips from start to finish, or use this alphabetical subject guide to help you find answers to your questions. (The index at the end of the book will help you locate even more specific information.)

Advertising

Computers

Correspondence

Credit Cards

Customers

Expanding

Tip 30   Move into a new combined home and office
Tip 31   Locate your business in a separate structure

Family and Friends

Tip 8   Don't assume that you can run a business and a household simultaneously
Tip 10   Keep your home space and work area separated
Tip 11   Hire your children or other family members to work for you
Tip 12   Enjoy being at home with your children
Tip 13   Share your dreams
Tip 22   Deal with occasional feelings of isolation
Tip 23   Keep in touch via the information highway

Getting Help

Tip 7   Know your own limitations, and delegate when necessary
Tip 8   Don't assume that you can run a business and a household simultaneously
Tip 11   Hire your children or other family members to work for you
Tip 51   Pay for worker's compensation insurance

Insurance

Tip 49   Carry adequate liability insurance coverage
Tip 50   Shop for business insurance on the Internet

Management

Marketing

Neighbors

Networking

Office Arrangement

Zoning

Tip 1

Analyze your personal rhythms

Whether your personal circadian rhythms—daily cycles of energy, followed by the need for rest—make you a morning person or a night owl, try to arrange your workday around them.

Granted, you sometimes have to meet clients on *their* terms, so you can't always have it your way. But you know when you are likely to be at your most creative and ready to take on the world, and when you should just vegetate or do no-brainer chores. Working within your personal rhythms isn't selfish—it makes you a more effective and pleasant person, which benefits your business endeavors as well as your personal relationships.

If you're a West Coast early bird, you can hit the deck in the wee hours and make those phone calls to people back East; then head for the beach in the afternoon, if you like. If you live on the East Coast, you can play golf during the day and make calls in the late evening, and still catch Californians during their working hours. If you're a Thomas Edison type and prefer to take frequent naps and then get back on the job refreshed, go right ahead. You can even adjust your hours seasonally, to take advantage of daylight-saving time and avoid driving in the dark.

Parents can schedule workaday tasks around family schedules; for example, attending your children's after-school sports events and then working for a couple of hours when everyone else in the household is settled down for the night. You might want to attend daytime workshops, classes, and seminars, but if they're scheduled at night, you can take a siesta during the day to make sure that you're wide-awake and can participate fully.

Most of us experience periods during the day when we don't feel energetic. Use those downtimes to do tasks that don't require much thought, such as opening mail and other routine chores.

As a home-based entrepreneur, you *are* your business. If you're like most of us, you work alone. Keeping yourself motivated and focused, energized and healthy, should be your paramount concerns. Whether they call themselves homebodies, home workers, or open-collar entrepreneurs, those who work at home call their own shots. They dress (or don't) as they please, schedule their time to suit themselves, and enjoy their choice of surroundings. One of the main reasons for having a business that is based in your home is the freedom to take advantage of whatever makes *you* tick.

Tip 2

Develop a daily routine

Some people can cope with working long hours for several days, or traveling a lot and having a varied schedule, but a regular daily routine seems to work best for most of us. Try to develop a pattern that works for you.

If you've worked nine to five most of your life, that may be the way to continue in your home workplace. If you develop the habit of going into your home office or workroom at the same time every day, you'll be less likely to let distractions keep you away from your work. You might choose to start your day by answering mail, sending e-mail, or making phone calls. By structuring your day's activities, you'll get more done.

When you have things to attend to out of your office, it might help to set aside one afternoon a week for making sales calls, picking up supplies, or running other errands. Even if your schedule changes drastically from day to day, plan each day's activities the night before or first thing each morning, to avoid unproductive time or a lack of direction.

Tip 3

Take frequent breaks during your workday

You can take breaks whenever you like, and eat lunch at any time—although many home-business folks say it's hard to resist snacking when it's so convenient! If you're on a special diet, it's often easier to stick to it at home instead of having to pack a lunch or eat out every day. Keep fresh fruit and healthy beverages handy to keep up your energy level.

If an exercise routine is part of your day, take time out for a swim or a run. You don't even have to change your clothes when you return to work—who cares if your hair is dripping wet from doing a few laps in the pool? Take a short walk, listen to some of your favorite music, or close your eyes and meditate. Read something unrelated to work, pick and arrange some flowers, or start preparations for dinner. For a change of scene, move your paperwork to a different location in the house or to the yard. Check up on the day's news or call a friend for a chat.

As you work, relax, but don't slouch. Change positions, and move from task to task so that you don't maintain the same posture for hours. Blink your eyes and stretch frequently. Even though your first-grade teacher told you not to fidget, you should squirm and wiggle—it relieves pressure in all your muscle groups. One of the great benefits of working at home is that you can stretch out on a sofa or on the floor for a few minutes, if that gets rid of the kinks. Besides, your dog or cat will probably appreciate the chance to command your attention and play for a few minutes. Many people find meditation a good relaxer, as well.

It's important to get up from your desk or workstation every hour or so to stretch and relax your muscles. Blink and look out the window to relieve eye strain. It's easy to get so involved in your work that you find yourself stiff and tired after too many hours in the same position. But be disciplined about it—you have work to do! If necessary, use a kitchen timer or an alarm clock to remind you to get back to business.

Tip 4

Make time for leisurely vacations

Michael and Jennifer Whitaker, owners of Spinning Jenny, a needlecraft business they run out of their home in Yorkshire, England, offered this advice: Design your business so that you don't have to be involved twenty-four hours a day, 365 days a year. Plan for weeks, or at least days off, or afternoons to go fishing. Remember that there will be occasional emergencies when you can't be at the helm, so your business has to be able to function without you. If it can't, things could fall apart in your absence.

Everyone needs a vacation, so a block of time away from it all should be factored into your calendar. View your time off as a reward for all your hard work. Your friends and family need your attention and the chance to spend some quality time with you, away from everyday pressures.

Find someone you trust who can fill in for you occasionally. In the bed-and-breakfast business, there are people who fill in exclusively; they don't operate their own establishments, but hire themselves out to run other people's inns so the owners can take vacations from their demanding, around-the-clock, customer-service enterprises. You might be able to find such "take-over" people through a network of home-based businesspeople like yourself, or via a newsletter or professional organization in your field. Or, consider training someone—an interested friend or family member—who can occasionally fill in for you. If this doesn't seem possible, you'll just have to hang out the "Gone Fishing" sign and shut down for a week or so.

Tip 5

Keep yourself healthy

Periodic physical checkups are important for everyone, but when the responsibility to get the job done is solely yours, it's even more critical for you to stay healthy. Common sense, a good diet and exercise program, and healthy habits are key. Pressure and deadlines may make it difficult for you to get enough rest, but don't try to work nonstop—that's when minor ailments like colds and flu linger on and on.

For anyone who suffers from occasional allergy flare-ups or other periodic aches and pains, working at home has the advantages of a controlled environment and readily available medication. Wearing comfortable clothes has its advantages, too. For those who work at home, every day is casual Friday. Sweats, jeans, shorts, or even pajamas may constitute your working wardrobe. And at home, there's no such thing as a bad-hair day.

James Hickey, a freelance photographer, understands the importance of staying healthy: "People hire *me*. They see my samples and they choose me to photograph their weddings and other important events. I have to be there, even if I'm sick."

Tip **6**

Practice stress management

Your emotional and mental health is just as important as your physical health. Learn to deal with stress, that all-too-prevalent modern-day malady. Taking breaks and vacations will help, but only if you know how to relax. It won't do much good to take a pleasure trip if you worry about your business the whole time you're gone, spend most of the time on the telephone checking up on business matters, and then get right back into the same old stress mode when you return.

Stress has been described as the "fight or flight" syndrome. Research links stress with such chronic conditions as hypertension; irritable bowel syndrome (IBS); coronary artery disease; depression; ulcers; tobacco, drug, and alcohol abuse; and eating disorders.

Your home office is your special place, an environment where you can enjoy music, wind chimes, or the sound of a soothing mini-waterfall. You can have an aquarium full of tropical fish, a cushion for Fido, or a cage for Tweety. Your child's playpen or crib can be part of your office décor. Favorite paintings, sculpture, and photographs can add color and visual interest. Your hobbies and collections can be attractively displayed and enjoyed every day.

Learn to relax, even if you think you don't have the time. Dean Ornish, president and director of the nonprofit Preventive Medicine Research Institute in Sausalito, California, says, "Busy people often think that relaxing means doing nothing—in other words, wasting time." He teaches that techniques such as meditation, stretching, deep breathing, visualization, and progressive relaxation can improve efficiency and productivity, not to mention the length and quality of your life.

For many home-business owners, the workload seems impossible. A survey by the U.S. Public Health Service estimated that 70 to 80 percent of Americans who visit their physicians each year are suffering from a stress-related disorder. Many of them are also part of the "sandwich generation," coping with the stacked responsibilities of taking care of elderly parents, their own children, and sometimes even their grandchildren.

Reed Moskowitz, medical director of Stress Disorders Medical Services at the New York University Medical Center, counts many owners of small businesses among his patients, and notes their "gung-ho, I can solve it" attitude. "Add to this the stresses of relationships and the lack of a personal life," Dr. Moskowitz explains, "and it's obvious that one of the most stressful occupations in the world is being the owner of a small business." Dr. Moskowitz advises to "keep things in perspective. Most entrepreneurs start their businesses to enhance their lives. Soon they may find that the business is running them, rather than them running the business. After all, what good does it do to have a successful enterprise if you end up in the coronary-care unit?"

Attend a stress-management seminar or workshop, or read a book on meditation or other relaxation techniques. Nischala Devi helps clients make their workplaces and homes more relaxing environments through her consulting service, Abundant Well-Being. She is the former director of stress management for the Dean Ornish Program for Reversing Heart Disease. The techniques Devi suggests include stretching and breathing exercises, many of which can be practiced while sitting at a desk or workstation, or even while you are talking on the telephone. (See Recommended Reading for books on relaxation and meditation.)

Tip 7

Know your own limitations, and delegate when necessary

Be realistic about what you hope to accomplish with your home-based business, and how much you can effectively deal with on your own. It might help to analyze the multiple tasks connected with running your business by making a list. List the things you do well in one column, and the things that give you trouble in another. You may want to take some courses in marketing or sales, computer basics, simple bookkeeping, or other subjects, if you feel you need to manage your whole operation yourself. But concentrate on your strengths, and capitalize on them. It's not always going to be easy, but self-confidence and a good dose of "I think I can, I think I can!" will take you a long way.

Dr. Moskowitz advises, "Realize there are limitations to your time and energy. . . . Focus on the need for balance in your life. While you may derive a lot of positive feelings from your business, you also need the nurturing of family and friends and involvement in something other than ambition."

Try to delegate or contract out the things that take too much of your time. If bookkeeping is not your forte, don't waste time doing it—the job will probably take you longer than it would a professional, so go ahead and hire someone else to do the job. Hire a salesperson to sell while you concentrate on your product or service. Hire seasonal help to get you over the hump when you're really busy. Consider bartering or trading your services with other home-based businesspeople in exchange for work you don't want to take on yourself.

Tip 8

Don't assume that you can run a business and a household simultaneously

While it's true that some household chores can be squeezed into a work-at-home day, it's not always easy to operate your business and be a supermom or superdad at the same time. Although many parents choose home businesses in order to spend more time taking care of their children, baby-sitters and child-care services are often required when the work just has to get done. Likewise, it's difficult to take care of housework if you are working long hours to make your business a success. Either let the nonessentials slide, or hire someone to help out.

Many working people take care of their elderly parents and in-laws, who sometimes require even more attention than young children do. Added to the burden is the sadness of seeing the decline of their health, vitality, and mental ability. Part-time elder care, or a trade-off with someone in a similar situation, can give you a breather and a chance to pamper yourself a little by taking an afternoon off or simply enjoying lunch with an understanding pal.

Just as a woman working at home shouldn't be expected to do all the housework, a man at home all day shouldn't be expected to be Mr. Fix-It. Again, it's important to set aside the time required for home maintenance. Or hire someone else to do those jobs.

Tip 9

Reward yourself occasionally

Don't forget to take a few hours at the end of the month or at the conclusion of your busy season to reflect on what you've accomplished, and celebrate! Sometimes the going gets tough, but chances are you've reached at least some of your goals, and that's a strong incentive to keep on trying.

If you plan ahead for a vacation, it will be something to look forward to when you're working on a major project. We all need a reason to keep ourselves motivated, so try to focus on something you'll be able to enjoy when the job is done. Treat yourself to a night on the town, or buy something special that you've been wanting—within reason, of course. It's a good idea to buy tickets to concerts or sports events ahead of time; if you have the tickets already, you'll probably make the effort to get out of the house.

When commitments overlap, there's not always time to rest between each one, but it's important to take a break if it's at all possible. If you can enjoy patting yourself on the back a bit, you'll be able to tackle the next project with enthusiasm. Sometimes we finish one job only to find that we're already behind schedule on the next one, and we feel as though we're on an endless treadmill of obligations.

Tip 10

Keep your home space and work area separated

First and foremost, your home is truly your castle. And nobody wants a castle that's cluttered and lacks personal space. This means that there shouldn't be business papers all over the dining-room table or unfinished products in mid-assembly in the family room—at least not all the time. Besides, this will probably result in misplaced files and sloppily built products.

If your business doesn't require much space, it probably won't be difficult to restrict it to a well-defined area that can be closed off at the end of each workday.

When clients and customers come to your home, it's best if you can devise a separate entrance to your office or showroom. If that's not feasible, figure out a way to divide spaces so that visitors don't feel that they are intruding on your space. If your house has an entry with a hallway leading to your office, put a screen across the hallway next to your office door to separate that area. This will serve as a temporary barrier that can be removed when you need the entire space.

The other members of your household need to know that when you are working, they're not supposed to interrupt unless it's an emergency. Explain your schedule, and tell them when you will be able to spend time with them. You may want to post a sign (for example, "Out to Lunch, Back at 1 P.M.") on your office door, indicating when you will be free.

Tip 11

Hire your children or other family members to work for you

There are tax breaks, as well as other benefits, in having family members work for you. Just be sure that whatever you pay them reflects the real value of work that they perform.

As of the year 2000, you can pay each of your children as much as $6,400 annually. You deduct their wages from your business income (reducing your own income tax, your Medicare tax, and, potentially, your Social Security tax). If your child takes the standard deduction and makes a contribution to an individual retirement account (IRA), he will pay no taxes at all on the income. If the business is a sole proprietorship or a partnership owned only by the parents, the wages of a minor child are also exempt from Social Security and Medicare taxes.

Many home-based entrepreneurs have also found that it's good training for children to participate and to learn what it takes to run a business. They grow to appreciate their parents' efforts on the family's behalf, and they learn where that hard-earned money actually comes from.

Mary Lee Huber of Michigan gave up her advertising agency when she became pregnant. She decided to turn her hobby—herbal crafts—into a career. With her sister, Alice Dunkel, whose daughter was born within ten days of Mary Lee's son, she made wreaths and arrangements in her basement and sold them at craft fairs. The two sisters shared child-care; and when the children started school, Mary Lee and Alice bought a nearby apple orchard and expanded their company, Wintergreen Herb and Potpourri, into a shop surrounded by gardens. Both children have spent a lot of time in their mothers' shop, and they sometimes sell blooms from their own flower stand on the premises to earn spending money.

Being paid for the work one does is more than just a monetary reward; it fosters self-worth and a sense of security and independence. We still remember how pleased Lou's eighty-year-old mother was when she helped us out with some clerical work. After having been retired and financially independent for several years, she enjoyed actually earning money for her secretarial skills.

Tip 12

Enjoy being home with your children

Home-based male entrepreneurs (who are the majority of home-based workers) express their satisfaction with being stay-at-home dads. Instead of waving good-bye every morning to those little tykes who seem to grow up overnight, they get to share in the daily lives of their children. They can allow time to be sports coaches and help with school projects. They can be there when children are sick, injured, or need special attention.

When Eric and Valerie Law's daughter was born, Valerie's employer didn't offer her the option of telecommuting, so when she returned to work after her maternity leave, Eric became a stay-at-home dad. They relied on part-time day care so Eric could get his academic-journal-editing work done and attend occasional business meetings, and it proved to be a workable and rewarding situation for all three of them.

Many moms become "mothers of invention" when their children are newborns, so they can spend time at home and still work at the careers they enjoy or launch new ventures. The Small Business Administration estimates that 60 percent of all businesses owned by women are started at home.

Gladys Castro is the owner of Unique Creations, a faux-finish and wall-sculpturing business she runs out of her West Coast home. Castro, a registered nurse who started her home business so she could be at home with her two young sons, founded the Women Entrepreneurs Network (WEN). The organization has a mailing list of 1,000, a Web site (www.womenentrepreneurs.com), and a newsletter, and holds monthly business seminars for working women. Her new business, www.Mammapreneurs.com, an online support and resource center for work-at-home mothers, is an affiliate of WEN.

Today's "mamapreneurs" are involved in much more than yesterday's merchandise-demonstration parties, craft shops, and seamstress businesses. They're taking advantage of the flexibility of working at home, and they have the skills and know-how to be successful. This trend has been fueled by women's frustration with the corporate world's glass ceilings, the difficulty of finding adequate day care, the desire to spend more time raising their children, and the enjoyable challenge of running a potentially profitable business. Many of the products and services these entrepreneurial women offer are the results of their own experiences as working mothers and their discovery of niche markets they feel they can serve. Web sites, literature, and networking support groups feed this growing subculture.

Tip 13

Share your dreams

You probably discussed your long-range plans with your family or housemates before you launched your home business. But you should still take time periodically to make sure everyone in the household is comfortable with having your business at home. Even if they don't participate in the work, there are always adjustments to be made, along with some sacrifices. Be prepared to swap roles when it comes to responsibilities such as child care and household maintenance. Tasks should be neither "yours" nor "mine"—instead, think of them as "ours." Assess your shared goals and dreams, and adjust them if necessary. And remember to let everyone close to you know that you appreciate all of their help and support.

Tip **14**

Do a periodic property assessment

As your home-based business grows, you should do an occasional analysis to make sure your house is still suitably located for your enterprise. It should be near—or easily accessible to—your prospective customers or clients, materials and equipment suppliers, technical-support and repair services, and consultants, such as your bookkeeper or accountant. If you think that your needs for these services might change in the foreseeable future, you might consider relocating. Of course, if you rent your home or apartment, this is more feasible than if you own your home.

If you are a manufacturer, you need to be able to ship your finished products to your customers as conveniently as possible. Do freight services such as United Parcel Service or Federal Express offer pick-up service in your locale? You might need to consider hiring a delivery service or making deliveries yourself. This could be a good job for someone else in your family, even on a seasonal or part-time basis. Rosemary Ward delivers flower arrangements during the wedding and holiday seasons and on Mother's Day for her daughter-in-law's West Coast floral-design business.

Employees and child-care providers might need to use public transportation to come to work at your home. You want to be sure that it's easy for them—as well as for clients and delivery people—to find your street. It should be well marked and easily accessed from major crossroads or highways.

Whenever you do need to drive around the community to run errands, it's helpful if you can accomplish several chores by making many stops in one outing. You should try to avoid long, unnecessary, or too-frequent trips. Make checklists and plan an itinerary ahead of time.

Tip **15**

Protect your business from weather, fire, and theft

If you live in a severe-weather or remote rural area, consider using e-commerce to market your product or service via the Internet. Or you could sell merchandise—either your own or someone else's—by catalog, phone, and/or mail order. You will need additional space for packaging and shipping goods. Some businesses, particularly Internet companies, actually have no inventory on their premises; they simply take orders and the goods are shipped from distributors elsewhere.

If your locale is subject to power interruptions, winter freezes, or any other vicissitudes of Mother Nature, you need to plan your business accordingly. You need business-interruption insurance or other contingency plans to tide you over in case of situations that would affect your enterprise. Be sure that your computer files are frequently backed up, and consider installing a generator to keep power available.

It goes without saying that you want a safe environment for your home, and this applies to any business location as well. Take an interest in your community's crime-protection, disaster-relief, and fire-fighting services, as well as the facilities for trash collection, street-surface and street-lighting maintenance, and snow clearance in the winter. Add outdoor lighting and keep your landscaping trimmed to provide visibility on your property so no one can lurk around or break in easily. In high-fire-risk areas, fire-abatement landscaping is sensible. And have a family evacuation kit and a disaster plan. After all, your family, your home, and your livelihood are at stake.

Protect your business from local-area circumstances that might cause you to suffer a business interruption or loss. Natural disasters such as earthquakes, floods, landslides, tornadoes, winter storms, and wildfires, as well as power or telephone outages, street closures, and construction obstacles, are conditions against which you must be prepared to defend your business. Be sure you have adequate business insurance, as well as homeowner's coverage. Consider installing a sprinkler system for fire protection, and a burglar-alarm system.

Tip 16

Travel smart

Do you often need to travel long distances in order to consult with your clients, work on sales promotions, attend trade shows, or buy inventory? If so, proximity to an airport, train station, or major highway system is important. You don't want to spend time traveling or driving that could be better spent in the development of your business.

But if you do need to travel long distances by car, train, or plane, try to use the time wisely. Take along reading material, make notes, use a cellular phone or laptop computer, or dictate into a tape recorder. Make your home office portable and take it with you.

Audio books on cassette tapes or CDs are available on topics such as current fiction, self-help, and motivation, and will help you make good use of your travel time.

The VIP lounges in major airports provide food and drinks, televisions and VCRs, telephones, fax and copy machines, and even handy office cubicles for using your laptop computer, tape recorder, or phone. Continental and Northwest airlines charge a $300 annual membership for the use of VIP facilities at any airport locations, any time. One-day memberships also are available, generally costing around $35. American Airlines' Dallas-Fort Worth Airport Admirals Club has a family area, new shower facilities, twenty-one work areas, and nine conference rooms that can seat fifteen to twenty people. In many clubs, members can make reservations and receive boarding passes, seat assignments, and flight information, instead of having to wait in the check-in line with dozens of other passengers. The Plaza Premium Lounge in Hong Kong, designed for economy-class passengers, offers showers, e-mail, a bar, a music-appreciation area, and a golf putting range, as well as standard business facilities, for a flat fee of $30 per visit.

Diners Club International offers its cardmembers free use of its airport lounges in forty-eight airports worldwide, including three at the Miami International Airport. Hotels and convention centers offer facilities that provide many of the same services as airport lounges.

Combat jet lag by getting plenty of sleep and eating light meals that include starches, carbohydrates, and greens. In flight, drink plenty of fluids, because in the air your body dehydrates at twice the normal rate. Avoid caffeine and alcoholic beverages, because they act as diuretics. Dress comfortably, and stretch or walk around the plane if you can. Set your watch to the new time zone. Yawn or chew gum to avoid pressure buildup in your ears. Melatonin, available as an over-the-counter drug, is a hormone that is secreted by our bodies when it's time to sleep; the release is triggered by the absence of light and the timing of meals. If used, it should be taken at nightfall when you reach your destination. (Note: Melatonin, which is available in health-food stores, has not yet received official approval from the Food and Drug Administration.) When you arrive at your destination, a long soak in the bathtub will help to rehydrate you. Try not to overbook yourself too soon after long-distance travel, when you might not be feeling alert and physically fit.

You can make good use of the time between flights or business appointments to take an invigorating walk or otherwise work out the kinks from sitting too long. Remember to give yourself frequent mental breaks; you can make a stop at a museum, zoo, or botanical garden for a change of scene.

When traveling in your car, have materials handy so you can take advantage of traffic delays, canceled or rescheduled appointments, and other unexpected blocks of time. Again, use some of the time to take breaks to stretch your legs—and rest your brain cells.

Keep track of business-related automobile mileage and expenses. For most commuters, the cost of traveling from home to work is not tax-deductible. However, self-employed people whose home office is their principal place of business can write off all business-related travel costs, such as mileage to a client's office from the home-office location. Leasing a car for business use is also a tax-deductible expense.

Tip 17

Capitalize on specialty products

Market unique local products to out-of-towners. Tourists tend to buy souvenirs that will remind them of their travels and local gifts for the "folks back home." If your community produces distinctive merchandise, you may find a strong market among visitors. It would be beneficial to publicize these products among agencies catering to tourists, such as local convention and visitors bureaus, chambers of commerce, and travel agencies.

Gift baskets are a good way to promote local products. Distinctive snack foods, cookies, cheeses, coffee mugs, books about local history or attractions, T-shirts, and caps are some of the items that could be included. The baskets could be provided for meeting and seminar attendees, or placed as welcoming gifts in hotel and motel rooms.

Such baskets were enjoyed by 300 journalists and businesspeople touring southwestern South Dakota, who found different gifts from the state's department of tourism in their rooms at Custer State Park each evening. They received buffalo sausages, knives and buffalo-shaped cutting boards; metal mugs with a buffalo design, packages of locally produced cocoa and "buffalo chip" cookies, buffalo-shaped metal business-card holders and picture frames, and fleece shirts featuring the logo of the buffalo roundup they attended. On the tourists' dinner tables, there were printed programs and menus with handmade-paper covers, table centerpieces made of local rocks and other natural materials, leather-thong-and-bead napkin rings, and booklets with buffalo-hide covers.

Tip 18

Take your show on the road

If you conclude that your location is not suitable for clients to come to you, think of mobilizing your business. Could you provide your service at the customer's site? Dog groomers, farriers (people who shoe horses), knife sharpeners, and housecleaners are among those who can work efficiently out of well-equipped vans or recreational vehicles. Customers enjoy the convenience of having service providers come to their doors.

Every weekend, Wayne and Jan Montano travel in their motor home to set up shop at major antiques shows, where they repair valuable cut glass and crystal. Another family member attends a one-day show each month, estimating repairs and bringing the damaged pieces to the Montanos' home workshop in rural California. After repairs are made, the antiques are delivered to the next month's show, where the owners pick them up.

James Hickey, a portrait photographer, doesn't work out of a studio; he prefers to pose people in their own home surroundings or in scenic outdoor settings at nearby parks. When James came to our home to take our picture, he suggested posing our collie pup with us. It never would have occurred to us to take the dog to a studio sitting.

Lots of businesses are based on working at the customer's home or business location. Examples are businesses offering interior decorating, building and contracting, plumbing, and other trades. Female entrepreneurs may have a unique opportunity in these types of service businesses. Carola Lindquist, whose business is called I Love to Wallpaper, says,

"Some women customers feel safer having a female tradesperson in their home."

Because of zoning laws and other home-business regulations, certain types of businesses that cannot be operated out of a home can be performed at the customer's location. In some states, for example, food cannot be prepared in a home kitchen for sale elsewhere, but it's perfectly legal for a personal chef to prepare food in the client's kitchen. Typically, the chef plans a menu for two weeks' worth of dinner entrées, shops for all the ingredients, and does the cooking in the client's kitchen. The prepared meals are frozen, and instructions for preparation and serving are included, plus menu suggestions to complete the meals. A chef might charge $275 for ten meals for two people, including the groceries, the preparation, and, of course, the cleanup.

Other professional chefs hire out for cooking parties. A meal-prep demonstration might cost $45 per person, including food but not wine. An all-day, hands-on class that includes a shopping trip to specialty markets and buying tips could cost two to four times as much, depending on the intricacy of the meal and the celebrity of the rent-a-chef.

Tip 19

Schedule meetings in places other than your home

The nature of many businesses requires calling on clients at their homes, shops, or offices, so it may not be necessary to arrange a home office for client visits. You could also consider setting up an appointment at a restaurant or other public place. This might be a safer place to schedule an initial meeting, if you are hesitant about having strangers come to your home.

If you need a private meeting room, there are other alternatives. Service centers such as Kinko's rent conference rooms in many of the companies' locations. You might be able to trade services with another businessperson in exchange for the occasional use of their conference room or office, or use the facilities at a Small Business Development Center (set up by the United States Small Business Administration). Many communities now have "incubators"—joint-use facilities for home-based or small-business entrepreneurs.

There is often an even more logical reason for meeting somewhere other than your home office. For an interior designer, a furniture, fabric, flooring, or tile showroom would be appropriate. A landscape architect might want to meet clients at a nursery, botanical garden, or horticultural center to discuss the clients' preferences in plants.

Tip 20

Be a good neighbor

In urban areas, local zoning ordinances and covenants, conditions, and restrictions (CC&Rs) of the homeowners' associations pretty much spell out what you can and can't do with your home business. Do your homework so you won't break any local regulations and run into nasty surprises down the road that might jeopardize your home-business setup.

Even if it isn't in the CC&Rs, you don't want to do anything that will aggravate the residents of your community. There must be adequate parking space—preferably off the street, rather than in front of others' homes—for clients or employees who come to your home, and for trucks making deliveries. Outdoor signage may be restricted; even if it isn't, make sure that your signs blend in with the neighborhood surroundings. And, of course, you can't do anything that will endanger anyone or lower your neighborhood's property values. You need to cultivate the good will of everyone with whom you come in contact—it will help your business thrive. They may be potential customers; they can also spread the word about your business to their friends, relatives, and business contacts.

Being on good terms with your neighbors doesn't mean that you are always available to accept package deliveries or keep tabs on their children, unless it is truly convenient for you to do so. Sometimes neighbors may try to take advantage of your being at home during the day, but you'll have to make it clear that you are *working* during whatever business hours you have established for yourself—conventional or otherwise.

Depending on the demands of your own business, you might consider expanding by offering services to your neighbors as a courtesy or for a reasonable fee. You could charge to accept deliveries, meet repairmen, or provide after-school day care. When your neighbors are out of town, you could feed and walk dogs, water plants and tend gardens, shovel snow, and see that mail and newspapers don't pile up. If you're handy, you could offer fix-it services in your neighborhood.

People working at home frequently encounter neighbors who just drop in for a visit because they know you are home. Again, stress that you are working, and let them know what time you will be free and when you would welcome a coffee break or a walk around the block.

Participate in a neighborhood watch or helping-hand safe-haven program, in which volunteers place signs in their windows to let young children know that they can come to them for help in emergencies. In any case, your neighbors will feel safer knowing that another resident is at home and aware of any unusual happenings. Likewise, you and your business will benefit from your neighbors' awareness of your home-based enterprise, because they will probably become protective of your property as well.

Tip **21**

Upgrade your address

Your address is part of your business image. If you use your actual home address, you can add a suite or office number to make it seem more like a commercial location. A community or subdivision name, such as Lang Ranch or Equestrian Trails, might lend elegance to your address. Just make sure it doesn't confuse your postal carrier.

It's generally better—and sometimes legally required on product labeling—for a business to have a full street address, rather than just a post-office box number. However, this will depend on your product, the type of clientele you are seeking, and whether you want to give the impression that you are a big or small operation. For your particular business, a post-office box may be quite all right. But you still need a specific location for United Parcel Service and Federal Express, which do not deliver to post-office boxes.

Another alternative is to use a commercial mailbox service or Associated Mail and Parcel Center (AMPC). However, whether you use a post-office box or a commercial mailbox service, you'll have to pick up your mail yourself, which can be an unproductive demand on your time.

Tip **22**

Deal with occasional feelings of isolation

Many home-based entrepreneurs, in rural areas as well as cities, sometimes experience feelings of isolation. It's easy to feel lonely and unconnected to the rest of the working world. The homebound, the physically challenged, or caregivers with young children or elderly family members to look after can begin to feel trapped, even though they enjoy the work they are doing at home. Set aside a regular time to chat on the phone or have some other stimulating human contact.

Stephanie Henry noticed that she was striking up conversations with sales clerks at the supermarket and other strangers after she launched her court-reporting business from her apartment. On days when she was home transcribing depositions for hours, she realized that she craved a little more human contact than she was getting. She made it a point to set aside a specific time during those days for telephoning or taking a break to visit friends.

If circumstances and distances permit, try to arrange a weekly luncheon meeting with pals or business acquaintances. Join professional organizations or your local chamber of commerce and attend meetings. Sign up for workshops at your local Small Business Development Center. Join a gym or a mall-walking group. Not only will you expand your horizons and relieve your feelings of isolation; you'll also be networking and gaining new contacts that could be extremely worthwhile.

Tip 23

Keep in touch with friends and colleagues via the information highway

The Internet allows people to correspond quickly with each other, no matter where they are located. With e-mail, you can send a note to someone when you have a spare moment; they aren't interrupted and can answer when they have time. With a scanner or digital camera, you can send photographs to friends and relatives, just as you would with regular mail. Several companies offer electronic greeting cards that can be sent with a click of your mouse. You don't even need a computer to send and receive e-mail; you can just type your message into a gadget called PocketMail that transmits and receives messages via telephone.

The advantage of online bulletin boards and chat rooms is that they operate around the clock, so even if your working hours don't permit phone conversations during certain times of the day, you can still communicate.

Tip 24

Claim the home-office expense deduction

Tax advantages for the business use of your home became even more liberal with the passage of the Tax Relief Act of 1997, effective with the tax year beginning January 1, 1999. This makes it possible for those who perform most of their work away from their home offices or workshops—such as caterers, consultants, and contractors—to claim the home-office deduction. It's estimated that four out of five home-office businesspeople perform their income-producing services at their clients' locations or elsewhere and use their home office primarily or exclusively for administrative purposes. The deduction was previously disallowed if the home was not the primary worksite. Now the home-office expense is allowable, if the office is critical to the running of the business, and there is no other principal business/office location.

The following rules, however, still apply:

- The home-office space must be used exclusively and regularly for a trade or business (monitoring your stock-market investments does not qualify, unless you are a broker or dealer in stocks), unless it is space devoted to the storage of inventory, a day-care facility, or a separate building. It can be a room or other separately identifiable space, but does not have to be marked off by a permanent partition.

- The home office must be your principal place of business, although you may conduct some business at other locations (for example, doing paperwork in a hotel room), and you may out-source some administrative activities, such as bookkeeping.

A home is defined as a house, apartment, condominium, mobile home, or boat. It also includes structures on the property, such as an unattached garage, studio, barn, or greenhouse. It does not, however, include any part of your property used exclusively as a hotel or inn.

If you use space on a regular basis for providing day care, you can deduct the business expenses for that part of your home—even if you use the same space for nonbusiness purposes—if you meet certain requirements.

Refer to Internal Revenue Service Publication 587: Business Use of Your Home (Including Use by Day-Care Providers) for more information. The IRS uses the following example, among others: A self-employed anesthesiologist works in three local hospitals, but uses his home office to schedule appointments, prepare for treatments and pre-sentations, maintain billing records and patient logs, satisfy continuing medical-education requirements, and read medical journals and books. His home office now qualifies for the deduction. Interestingly enough, it was an anesthesiologist in this same situation who challenged the denial of his home-office deduction and caused the U.S. Supreme Court to rule in favor of the new, more liberal definition for business use of a home office.

Tip 25

Study the tax breaks for day-care providers

A home business that provides day care for children, the elderly, or other people who are unable to care for themselves is entitled to deduct the expenses related to the business use of the home. Under state law, you must have a license or other certification as a day-care center or family or group day-care home, unless your business is exempt.

If the part of your home that is used for day care is used exclusively for that purpose, you may deduct all the allocable expenses, subject to the deduction limit established by the IRS. However, if the use of part of your home as a day-care facility is regular but not exclusive, you must determine how often you actually use it for business. You may also use the area occasionally for personal reasons.

Again, refer to Internal Revenue Service Publication 587 for more information.

Tip 26

Think ahead about business-expense deductions

Direct expenses, expenses incurred exclusively for the business portion of your home—such as painting, cleaning, or repairs—are deductible. *Indirect* expenses are part of the expense of running your entire home, such as insurance and utilities. These expenses are deductible based on the percentage of your home used for business.

However, you may not deduct expenses for the parts of your home not used for business, such as your lawn, even though such expenses can add to the attractiveness of your business-related property.

Talk to your tax adviser or accountant to find out what portion of your household-upkeep expenses may be deductible, and keep records of all the expenses that might be allowed.

Another recent change in tax allowances was an increase in the Section 179 deduction. If you bought certain property to use in your business, you may be able to deduct (rather than depreciate) all or a part of its cost. For the year 2000, the total you can elect to deduct has increased to $20,000.

Tip 27

Find the right spot for your office

Although the most logical places for home offices are usually spare bedrooms, attics, garages, or basements, other spaces can be adapted as well. Like many of us, you may have set up your home office in what appeared to be the only space available. But maybe it doesn't quite work. Take a good hard look to see if it can be improved in terms of functionality and comfort. Do you have a large enough work surface? Is the lighting adequate? Does the color scheme make you feel energized and ready to work? If the budget allows, should you invest in some storage, shelf space, or other items to make your workspace more efficient?

These days, many families use their formal dining rooms only on special occasions, so adding built-ins or an armoire to house a computer and desk may be a practical idea. When the dining room is needed for dining, the office can be hidden from sight. A storage closet, loft, sun-room, butler's pantry, stair landing, or breezeway may provide enough space for an office or, at least, a workstation.

The minimum area needed to accommodate a work surface and maneuvering room for a chair is about 30 square feet. The work surface should be about 60 × 30 inches, with 25 to 30 inches of clearance beneath it. Fax machines and printers on rolling trolleys can be kept under the desk.

A room can be subdivided by a partial wall or a screen to separate its functions. You could combine an office with a home gym, and you'd have a built-in stress-relief setup! College students and designers of children's rooms have taken the loft idea to new heights, putting sleeping platforms (where ceilings are high enough) above study and activity areas to make the space do double duty.

A wet-bar alcove left over from the '70s might be just the space to convert into a home office. Most of these bars already have shelves and cupboards, and perhaps the counter space could serve as your desktop. Shutters that separate the bar from the adjacent family room will also serve to hide the clutter when you're in the middle of a project.

Carlin Guarnieri, an interior designer, suggests, "It's important to create a sense of space as different from the other parts of the house as possible." Different flooring material, paint colors, and furniture may help to accomplish this sense of separation and establishment of an area dedicated to working. Light colors for walls, floors or carpeting, furniture, and fabrics will make a room seem larger; dark colors produce a more intimate atmosphere. Choose tones that make you feel alert and productive.

However, if you prefer an office that doesn't look too different from the rest of your home décor, the manufacturers of home-office furniture have designed items, such as computer workstations, that resemble period pieces and blend nicely with other furnishings. A rustic table or antique desk functions just as well as a desk from the office-furniture store and might look more "at home" in your room. Utilitarian items such as computer drives, printers, scanners, and other equipment can be concealed behind cupboard doors, curtains, or screens if you prefer an unobtrusive workspace.

In the 1960s, Anne Emery wrote several books for and about teenagers in a tiny office that started as a closet tucked under the stairway of her family's two-story home. The small space was just big enough to accommodate her desk, chair, and typewriter. With the door open, she could keep track of family activities; with it closed, the room was a quiet place where she could concentrate on her work. And when she wanted to leave papers all over the desk, shutting the door made the room invisible.

Ralph and Terry Kovel are the authors of more than sixty-five books that have become staples in the antiques and collectibles field. They also write newspaper and magazine columns, publish a national newsletter, and appear on television. The Kovels operate their business from their home, which has been designed to include work areas for themselves and several employees—as well as display and storage space for their ever-growing antiques collection.

When Carol Amish of California was house-hunting, she fell in love with a model that had an oversized laundry room with plenty of storage cabinets for the inventory and files she needed for her business as a party-plan housewares dealer. In Ohio, Mary Hurlburt also located her home office in her laundry room, where she compiled newsletters on her computer for a number of local businesses. With four preschool children at home, she had plenty of loads of laundry to wash and dry every day.

Tip 28

Make your clients feel welcome

If clients or customers come to your home, you need adequate parking space, a separate entrance if possible, and a comfortable place where you can sit and converse. There should at least be an area where you can meet that is separate from household activities. Both your clients and the members of your household will be more comfortable if their privacy is assured. And it goes without saying that you want to eliminate interruptions and distractions.

Even minor remodeling can make a major difference in convenience. A separate entry door for clients who come to your home, or just as a means of removing yourself from household distractions, can provide separation and give you a more productive work environment.

It is best to have a space in or near your office that is large enough for two comfortable chairs, or at least for a single guest chair near your desk. A chair that you can sit in when you don't need to be at your desk is also a bonus for you when you are reading or taking a break.

If you have a coffee bar or refrigerator nearby, you will be able to offer refreshments without disturbing your housemates. Likewise, an adjacent bathroom for your clients' use will keep them away from household traffic.

Tip 29

Consider remodeling your home to accommodate your business

Is the space you're using as an office, studio, or workshop adequate for the needs of your growing business? Or do you find your work activities and materials overflowing into other areas of your home?

Adding windows, skylights, and better lighting and ventilation can improve cramped surroundings, especially in a garage, attic, or basement.

And if you decide to make any type of structural change, be sure to consider the allowable IRS deductions for business use of the home *before* you start your project.

Brion Jeannette, an architect, says that at least 75 percent of his clients request home-office space when they hire him to build or remodel their homes. According to a 1998 survey by Wirthlin Worldwide, slightly more than 31 percent of U.S. households had dedicated some of the space in their residences to a home office. A substantial number of these offices were used for full-time home-based businesses.

Whether you are remodeling or building new space, consider sound insulation for the home office. Solid-core doors and insulation for the walls and ceiling are recommended. You can also add an extra layer of gypsum drywall board to the walls and ceiling inside the office and to the shared walls of any adjacent rooms. You could also put neutral rooms, such as bathrooms and closets, between your office and the rest of the house. If modifications don't solve noise problems entirely, consider a white-noise machine to mask still-audible sounds.

Many contemporary residential floor plans include a room located near the front entrance, sometimes with its own door leading to the outside. Generally, there is an adjacent bath. Aside from being well situated for a home office, these rooms can also be adapted for use as dens, guest rooms, or maid's quarters.

When Martha and Bill Weiler designed their new home in Idaho, they chose a compact one-bedroom home. It has a library/office for Bill and a tucked-away smaller office for Martha. To accommodate visitors, they built a guest wing with two bedrooms and a bath. The wing is separated from the main house by the garage, yet joined to it by a covered porch. Martha is a freelance book editor, and uses the guest wing as an office where she and an assistant have room to do their work comfortably.

When we first purchased our home several years ago, we experimented with furniture placement and decided that the small den off the front hallway was inadequate for large furniture or television viewing, which the living room and family room accommodated anyway. So, we planned to buy ready-made shelving and computer desks to make the den into a home office. After shopping for separate pieces of furniture, we contacted a local carpenter for an estimate on custom-made built-ins. He designed two computer desks and shelving on two walls for books and storage. The cost wasn't much more than we would have spent on ready-mades, and we saved some of the expense by finishing the pale-oak built-ins ourselves. The built-ins are much more attractive than ready-mades would have been, and they make better use of the available square-footage.

Our office is becoming overrun with the space requirements of our mail-order gourmet-food business—which at some future date we will probably subcontract out. There just isn't enough room for packaging merchandise for mailing. We need a work surface to wrap and box outgoing shipments, and we need storage for the necessary packing materials. This activity has been moved to a guest bedroom, which is inconvenient when we have overnight guests.

The answer might be a multifunction workroom with temporary shelves for storage and a large worktable. It could be part of the garage or combined with a laundry area. If the day comes when shipping activity is moved out of our home, we could simply reconfigure the space to accommodate a crafts workshop or storage area.

Tip 30

Move into a new combined home and office

If you need to expand your home-based business and need more space, consider moving to a new home. DeVaux McLean needed more room for his growing home-based telecommunications business, ProDial Communications, Inc. He was hooked on the convenience of working at home and being able to provide his customers with nearly twenty-four-hour service. After researching the costs of leasing a commercial site, furnishing and moving into it, and the other expenses involved in maintaining an outside office, he decided it would be more cost-effective to put the money into a newer, larger house. His new home now has enough space for a two-office business suite and his two full-time employees.

Paul and Sarah Edwards, authors of several books on self-employment, have moved their combined home and office twice to accommodate the needs of their family and their business. They now enjoy the beautiful scenery of Pine Mountain from their Fraser Park, California, home base.

Tip 31

Locate your business in a separate structure

Consider building or adapting a separate structure on your property in which you can house your office or manufacture and store your products. Expenses for a separate structure used solely for business purposes are entirely tax-deductible.

A detached garage, barn, garden shed, or other outbuilding might serve your purpose, if zoning ordinances permit such usage. Of course, depending on the requirements of your business, you might need to install electrical wiring or telephone lines. One of the main advantages of this arrangement is that you actually leave your house to go to work, and this can help your concentration. It's the "out of sight, out of mind" approach—members of your household can't make demands upon you if you aren't quite so accessible.

Builder and landscape architect Jeff Powers installed an office in the branches of a client's backyard sycamore trees. The treehouse suite features a motorized stairway that lowers at the press of a button. The fanciful and functional suite has all the amenities—a computer, conference area, kitchenette, and gas fireplace. It was built in San Juan Capistrano, California, more than ten years ago at a cost of about $130,000. Admittedly, this is an extreme example that could only work in a mild-climate area, but maybe it will get you thinking of solutions you never thought of before!

Elizabeth Gibson, an Oklahoma baker, built a second kitchen in a separate building to house her catering business, specializing in wedding cakes and desserts. Because she required a zoning variance for doing business in a residential area, she went door-to-door visiting neighbors prior to the zoning-board hearing, introduced herself, distributed sample pastries, and collected signatures approving her plans. The variance sailed through.

Elizabeth installed freestanding stainless-steel worktables, appliances, and floor drains. The building has high, peaked ceilings, skylights, French doors, and a half-bath that can be expanded later into a full bath. These features will make it easy to convert the building into living space, such as a guest house or family room, at some time in the future. This kind of a design could work just as well for an artist's studio or workshop.

The bakery's workspace is linked to the family's home by an attractive wooden deck with an outdoor play area, so Elizabeth can oversee her children's activities while she is working. A former caterer, she was often away from home evenings and weekends. Now clients come to her home to pick up their orders, and she has more time to spend with her family.

One new housing development in our area has a separate building on each homesite, which can be used as a guest house, an office/workshop or family activity area, or a three-car garage. Local zoning laws may prohibit you from installing a kitchen in such a building, because it could then be used as a separate rental dwelling. Martha and Bill Weiler have a guest house with a sink, refrigerator, coffeemaker, toaster oven, and microwave, but they could not equip it with a stove because of zoning restrictions. Some communities, however, allow "granny flats" where the homeowners' parents may live.

Tip 32

Arrange your workstation ergonomically

Ergonomics is the study of how people and machines work together. If your office furniture is mostly hand-me-downs and make-do improvisations, that's okay. But at least make sure you have a comfortable chair that places your body in the correct position for whatever type of work you do. Proper posture is worth spending some of your hard-earned dollars on. People who don't sit in supportive chairs that are adjusted to their tasks risk a number of physical problems, from fatigue to backaches to carpal-tunnel syndrome.

Your chair should be positioned to relate properly to your work surface and the equipment you use, such as your computer screen and keyboard, the tools on your workbench, or your drafting board. You need to be able to sit with both feet on the floor; use a footrest if your chair is too high. Your knees should extend just beyond the edge of your seat, and your lower back should be supported by the chair's backrest. If the seat is too deep for you to sit this way, use a cushion to move yourself forward in the chair. The chair's back should be vertically adjustable, to fit the natural curve of your lower back.

Place your computer monitor as far away from you as is comfortable. The top of the screen should be at eye level or slightly below to prevent your having to constantly tilt your head upward or downward. If you wear bifocal or trifocal lenses, you may need to lower the monitor even more, or get special glasses. Raise the monitor if you need to, or adjust your chair to compensate. Consider using a two-height desk surface with a lower level or pullout tray for your computer keyboard and an upper-level surface for writing, telephoning, and other tasks.

Your keyboard and mouse should be positioned together in front of you, low enough so that your forearms form a comfortable right angle when you type and move the mouse. Keyboards are available in several configurations, including curved shapes to keep your wrists at a natural angle. Your fingers should strike the keyboard flatly, without arching. A wrist rest will also take strain off your wrists as you type.

Don't crook your neck to hold a telephone against your shoulder—get a shoulder cradle or a headset, or switch to a speakerphone.

To complement the placement and comfort of your desk, computer, and chair, be sure that you have adequate lighting. Task lighting that falls where it's most needed is important, as is overall indirect light to wash the room and prevent pools of bright light surrounded by dimness, which is hard on your eyes.

Computer screens should be positioned so that window light doesn't reflect off them. In our office, the only space available for one of the computer monitors is in front of a window, so we hung two layers of dark-blue curtains, full-length over café-length, to give adequate shade. For just a few hours a day, the sun streams in, and all the curtains can be closed. At other times, we can open one or both sets completely. It's nice to be able to look out the window toward the yard and the sky.

Other helpful accessories are an anti-glare screen and a document holder that attaches to the side of the monitor to position material you are typing from.

Tip 33

Give yourself a dose of feng shui

Feng shui ("wind and water") is an ancient Asian art that provides formulas for the placement of a home on its site and for the design of the home itself. It can be applied to smaller spaces also, such as individual rooms and offices.

Kirsten M. Lagatree, author of *Feng Shui at Work*, explains that the objective of feng shui is to maximize the influences that bring good luck and prosperity. The influence of *chi*, or life force, is central to the practice of the art. It is thought that chi is attracted by light, water, living beings, plants, reflections, movement, bold colors, crystals, and art.

What's striking about feng shui is that it incorporates common-sense design principles that most of us have already learned in the environments in which we've lived and worked—principles that come second-nature to good interior designers and architects. Louis Sullivan, the famed Chicago architect, coined the term "Form follows function." Since you're combining two environments—home and office—it's critical to bring them into harmony.

If your home office is part of your kitchen, you have the advantage of having both fire and water nearby, and this is considered beneficial in feng shui. But kitchens can be centers of distracting activity, and heat and moisture might be harmful to sensitive computer equipment. On the other hand, having your office in a corner of your bedroom is thought to be a bit risky, because you don't want to bring a lot of energy into a room that needs to be a place of repose. If you must use bedroom space, Lagatree suggests using a room divider, an area rug, or a raised platform to separate the office from the sleeping area. Any room that is too crowded by a desk or other furniture blocks the circulation of chi. Mirrors and crystals can help increase the sense of space, and their reflective quality enhances the flow of chi.

Lagatree points out that piles of clutter in your home office interfere with the flow of chi; she quotes Barbara Hemphill, organizational guru and author of *Taming the Paper Tiger:* "A cluttered desk indicates a pattern of postponed decisions." There's certainly nothing mystical about that! Once you've cleared your desk of clutter, you can place special objects on and around it to focus power on important ideas and goals. Perhaps that is why so many of us have photos of friends and family in our offices.

The shape and size of the desk and its orientation in the room are also considered in the practice of feng shui. Rectangular or curved desks are good, but the common L-shaped desk and attached return need to be balanced by a plant, wastebasket, or other solid object across from the notch to square off the meat-cleaver shape of the work surface.

Adequate lighting that's not too harsh is also recommended, as are colors that bring harmony and peace. Birds, fish, and animals are a soothing presence. Healthy plants contribute to a positive environment by extracting carbon dioxide from the air and adding oxygen to it. Again, isn't this all just a dollop of common decorating and organizational sense?

Lagatree's book closes with this caveat: "Feng shui isn't magic. Invoking its ancient wisdom is no substitute for dealing with practical realities like balancing your checkbook. . . . Don't think of the practice of feng shui as moving furniture. Think of it as rearranging your life, from the inside out."

If these concepts interest you, there are expert practitioners and many books to consult on the subject.

If feng shui isn't your cup of tea, consider consulting an interior designer who specializes in home offices. Ask for referrals from the American Society of Interior Design or the International Interior Design Association, or examine some of the books on the subject included in our Recommended Reading list.

Tip 34

Invest only in office equipment that you really need

Michael LeBoeuf, Ph.D., author of a book and audio cassette called *The Perfect Business: How to Make a Million from Home with No Payroll, No Debts, No Employee Headaches and No Sleepless Nights*, cautions, "Make efficient use of smart tools. Information technology is a two-edged sword. Used wisely, computers, cell phones, voice mail, fax machines, beepers, telecommunications, all the wonderful tools of the information age can help make you rich by multiplying your value and productivity. Used wrongly, they will suck the time out of your life and add needless overhead to your business. So before you invest time and money in new technology (or anything else), ask yourself the following three questions: Will this help make me more sales? Will it lower my overhead? Will it enable me to get more done in less time? If the answer to all three questions is 'no', don't buy it or learn how to use it."

Think twice about purchasing equipment that may be needed infrequently. Stand-alone fax machines are becoming less necessary with the advent of faxes that are built into computers. But if you need to send or receive copies of articles or graphics, you will still need a conventional fax machine.

A fax machine can also do double duty as a copier. Photocopy machines are often the largest users of electricity in offices, so if you only need single copies, a dual-function fax machine will save you energy and copier costs.

If you only need a particular piece of equipment occasionally, consider renting, leasing, or using coin-operated machines available at a copy center, library, supermarket, mail center, or elsewhere. Compare the costs of the various options. If you don't need this equipment on a regular basis, owning it may not be cost-effective. These mechanical marvels may also be subject to expensive and time-consuming breakdowns and repairs, so you need to factor in the cost of maintenance contracts and service, as well as their anticipated useful life. You will save space in your home office by keeping equipment to a minimum.

Tip 35

Design your storage pieces to function

Cabinets or shelves for storage should have compartments or drawers that are easy to access, where items are visible, not hidden. If you can use a closet or a large cabinet, open bins are fine—you can see everything at a glance, and yet the doors, when closed, hide the clutter. Sliding and adjustable shelves are handy, as are various hanging storage systems.

Look for furniture or units that can be adapted, if you don't want to invest in commercial office furniture or you find it too ugly for home use. Kitchen cabinets may work just fine. If your storage needs are minimal, try an armoire with some attractive boxes or baskets inside to keep papers organized, or an attractive chest of drawers. Esther Spens uses a tall lingerie chest with a dozen shallow drawers to organize card files in her home office in Michigan. Julia Frand has an antique oak general-store spool chest with wide, shallow drawers where she stores beads and buttons for her craft business in Minnesota. Dental cabinets, hutches, and other antique pieces add character to a room and provide storage as well.

Our front-hall closet, not needed for coats in our mild climate, now houses a take-apart plastic shelf unit that holds all kinds of business supplies, packaging materials, and the like. It is handily located across the front hall from our home office.

When we remodeled our kitchen, we discussed cabinets with doors and pullout shelves with a friend who'd recently installed some. She pointed out that it takes two motions to use such sliding shelves. First you must open both of the doors completely, and then you can pull out the shelf. The open doors require a lot of swing-out room, especially in tight corners. Thanks to our friend's insight, our kitchen has lots of wide, deep drawers for bulky items, and only the tall pantry cabinet on the end wall has doors and pullout shelves. We're in the habit of leaving the doors open when we're cooking so we can grab ingredients and put them back easily. The same basic idea could be applied to any type of work-station. Open shelving is accessible, but not always attractive.

The design we envisioned for our home office included built-in storage consisting of L-shaped open shelving across two walls, plus some lateral file drawers and another bank of drawers for small office supplies. Our con-tractor, who himself is a home-based businessman, suggested putting cabi-net doors on the bottom tier of shelves so that unattractive items could be kept out of sight. And we left the area between the top of the cabinets and the ceiling open—that's where our collection of vintage toys is displayed.

Tip 36

Make yourself as accessible as possible

Offer a toll-free number, and publicize it in all your advertising, as well as on your letterhead and other printed material. If your competitors have toll-free numbers and your customers are often far enough away to incur toll charges when calling you, it's a good idea. You can save money by restricting the service to a defined local area, if you don't need national or international coverage.

Have enough telephone lines to receive incoming calls quickly. You may want to subscribe to an answering service, where real people can provide callers with basic information about your business and make appointments for you. Be sure to monitor the service to make sure that customer calls are being answered promptly and courteously.

If you must use an answering machine, be sure to make time to answer the calls that come in when you are unavailable. Have a voice-mail message that identifies your company, states the date, and lets callers know when to expect your reply. Encourage callers to leave information about their inquiry, so you can be prepared when you call them back. We've all played "phone tag," where we return someone's call only to get *their* answering machine, and no information has really been exchanged. When leaving a message for a caller, be explicit about the information you need, and ask the party to supply it by return call, even if they have to leave you another message.

A pager/beeper and/or cellular phone will allow clients to reach you any time they need to. Especially if you travel extensively, these gadgets can certainly keep you in touch, both with customers and your home office. It's getting quite common to see people shopping, driving, and going about other activities with their cell phones plastered to their ears. Remember, however, that there are some situations in which making or accepting calls is inappropriate, such as during lunch with clients.

Use call-forwarding or call-waiting to handle incoming calls if you are away from your office or busy on another line. It's useful to have a phone with "transfer" and "hold" buttons. "Caller ID" is another handy feature. Your telephone service provider will be more than happy to discuss the various options available in your area.

Speakerphones may be useful in a traditional office, but in a home office they can pick up domestic noises; in this case, you may want to use a "mute" feature. Another alternative is to use a lightweight headphone with a small mouthpiece, for hands-free convenience.

Tip 37

Give 'em the straight fax

Via fax-on-demand, your answering machine gives callers the option of pressing a button to receive a fax with your price list or other product information.

Sending information by fax costs less than calling someone on the telephone. You can send faxes any hour of the day or night. It doesn't interrupt people who are busy, yet it draws attention and usually elicits a quick response.

Martha Weiler sends out questionnaires so companies can submit product information for the annual buyers guide she edits. Faxing during nighttime hours, when long-distance telephone rates are low, costs far less than postage. If the questionnaires were mailed, a postpaid return envelope would have to be included at additional cost. But companies respond quickly and fax the information back at their own telephone expense. As Martha says, "Which gets your attention quicker—a letter or a fax placed on your desk?"

Tip 38

Take advantage of the time your customers spend on hold

While people are waiting to be connected to you or your customer service representative, provide something for them to listen to. The Maine

Office of Tourism uses instrumental music that features the cry of a loon. The CD, *From ME to You*, sets a mood for prospective visitors to the state. An outfitter or tour guide could also use music with a nature theme. Naturally, musicians or other performers should use recordings that showcase their talents. Some people find it irritating or even offensive to be forced to listen to talk radio, gospel music, or religious programming, so be selective.

Take the opportunity to tell callers about your company and its products. Provide your location and mailing address, or give your Web site address and suggest that callers visit for more information about you.

Your message can mention special promotions or new products. If it's appropriate for your type of product or service, you can offer a health tip or a "thought for the day." The idea is to make use of the time while your customer is on hold to convey useful information and make them willing to wait just a bit longer for their call to be answered.

Tip 39

Use conference calling and video conferencing

Conference calls can link several parties in a telephone conversation, enabling them to ask questions and exchange ideas almost as readily as they could in person. Video conferencing is a video phone call during which users see people and products on a screen in addition to being able to speak back and forth. These technologies eliminate travel time and expense by providing instant conferencing capability. It is also usually easier to set up an electronic meeting than to find a time convenient for all parties to get together. In some communities, facilities for video conferencing can be rented as needed at small-business centers or incubators.

Consult your local telecommunications company for advice; they can explain the types of services available in your area.

Tip **40**

Invest in equipment

These days, computers seem to be obsolete almost as soon as they are taken out of their shipping crates. New innovations seem to crop up every hour. But most businesses can't afford not to take advantage of this technology, for everything from word processing and record-keeping to communicating via the Internet.

Get more capacity (RAM) than you think you will need. You'll probably end up using more than you expected to. Try to decide in advance what functions you will require from your computer, such as composing correspondence, business management, spreadsheets, banking, and record-keeping. Beyond that, your particular business needs may require much more complicated programs if you will be doing extensive word processing, desktop publishing, architectural and interior design layouts, graphic design, or even music composition. You'll need software programs and the hardware to back them up. Sign up for local tech support right away. You can't afford to be stranded if your computer gives you problems.

Invest in a high-quality laser color printer. Chances are you will find more applications for it than you expected to. It will enable you to use a desktop-publishing program for professional-looking statements, stationery, flyers, and newsletters.

Scanners enable you to copy and e-mail graphics, photos, and draw-ings. Freelance photographers can send samples of their work instead of shipping valuable original slides or transparencies. Designers can transmit their ideas in the form of sketches and examples. You can use a digital camera to send electronic photos of finished projects or other three-dimensional objects to prospective customers.

Long-distance travelers, and others whose businesses require them to be on the road a great deal, find laptop, notebook, subnotebook, and palmtop computers convenient.

Have a tape backup, an external hard disk (such as a Zip drive), or some other means to store your work, and make it a habit to frequently save data. Some day when you least expect it, your hard drive may crash, taking all that valuable information with it.

Tip 41

Make use of computer programs for desktop publishing

Instead of typing ordinary letters and contracting out printing and graphic design, consider doing your own desktop publishing; a variety of programs are available to help you. You could put together a monthly or quarterly newsletter for your customers and produce your own promotional mail-ings, labels, postcards, and stationery. A real-estate agent could design flyers to attach to the "For Sale" signs on his listings. Copywriters could design brochures and direct-mail pieces for their customers. Price lists, price tags, "how to use" instruction sheets and booklets, mail-back response cards, questionnaires, and all types of enclosures for your regular mailings can reinforce your company's image every time you correspond with customers and prospects. You can generate your own presentation folders, customized proposals, and reports. If publishing is your main occupation, you can produce books, magazines, manuals, and directories.

Desktop publishing also requires high-quality printers, large-screen monitors, versatile scanners, and even digital cameras, as well as a storage system of hard drive(s), floppy disks, or Zip disks. Since desktop-publishing software requires a lot of memory, you'll have to purchase a system that's able to handle all your software.

Software programs such as ReadySetGo, QuarkXPress, Ventura Publisher, and FrameMaker are all designed to do word processing and page layouts. Drawing, painting, and illustration programs, and image-editing software that enables you to modify photographs and other images are also available. MacDraw, MacPaint, Adobe Illustrator, and Adobe Photoshop are used for these applications.

Naturally, unless you have the time and training to devote to desktop publishing, you might be better off using freelancers. Copy service centers offer assistance and have designers who will work with you on your projects.

Tip 42

Connect your home business to the Internet

Locate a reliable Internet service provider. Pricing is competitive. If you travel and require service away from home, be sure your provider offers local access numbers in other cities.

At least two dedicated lines are usually recommended for a business: one for voice communication and the other for faxing and Internet connections. A new service available in some areas provides a hookup via a cable modem (the same cable that's used for cable television) or a digital subscriber line (DSL), which is permanently hooked up to a telephone line for instant Internet access, eliminating the dial-in time formerly required.

The Internet is an invaluable research tool, with resource material on every conceivable subject. It may take you a while to get the hang of doing a concise search, but once you learn to narrow your criteria, it works like a charm. Pick keywords that will eliminate irrelevant sites. Learn to use Boolean operators, such as NOT, AND, OR, or AND NOT. Different search engines (AltaVista) and directories (Yahoo) or combinations of the two (Excite) have different ways of organizing Web sites. You might want to use all of them. Our current favorite is Dogpile, which searches a number of other search engines and directories. Use the HELP option to learn how to structure your search on a particular search site.

Be sure to evaluate the publisher of a site before you use the information you find; a lot of misinformation and self-serving propaganda is out there. One way to judge a source is by its domain type, which usually appears at the end of the main string of the Web address. The most common are:

- **com** Originally intended for a commercial entity. Now anyone can register a dot-com domain name. Many dot-coms are businesses, but individuals can also be represented this way.

- **edu** An educational institution or organization. While much of the information on such a site may reflect the school's credibility as a source, individual students and faculty members may have their own pages on the school's Web server.

- **gov** A branch of the United States government, or a state government. These are some of the most reliable sources of information.

- **mil** A U.S. military entity or NATO.

- **net** Entities and organizations that are part of the Internet's infrastructure, such as an Internet service provider. These sites may be provided for individual subscribers at little or no cost, so they are only as credible as the subscriber himself.

● **org** Usually a noncommercial organization, such as a not-for-profit group. Information found there may be accurate, but remember that some organizations have social or political agendas.

Shop for bargains on the Internet. Although people at first were skeptical about the security of using credit cards and buying via the Net, it has become one of the fastest-growing segments of worldwide commerce. You can compare prices and shop without leaving home.

Tip **43**

Establish your own Web site

It's been said that having a Web site is almost as demanding as opening a branch office or store. It must be monitored and frequently updated so that customers will want to visit often to see what's new. Customers can place orders at your Internet site. You can contract with another company to process credit-card orders if you don't want to open your own merchant account.

Lilah Valdiva has an on-line showroom and catalog where customers can view Egyptian Pillow Palace décor items and place their orders. Public Eye, a service that monitors Internet transactions and provides customer feedback, issued Lilah's Web page as a "registered safe shopping site."

Even if you don't sell your product directly on your Web site, you can provide an electronic showroom. Jim Robertson, a specialty landscaper whose company installs waterfalls and landscape features, shows photos on his Web site of jobs he's done, which gives prospective clients an idea of what he can do for them.

Free Web sites are available, as are pages that can be connected to the sites of organizations to which you belong. If you aren't ready to design your own, find a Web-site designer in your area who will do it for you. One thing to remember is that extensive graphics, animation, or sound effects on a Web site take time to load, and some users who access your site won't be willing to wait.

If you provide links to other sites, you may be able to collect a "finders fee" from them.

Tip 44

Use e-mail for business correspondence

Like faxing, e-mail is cheaper than phoning, doesn't interrupt people, and tends to elicit a prompt reply. You can use it twenty-four hours a day, and people can respond when it is convenient for them.

Your e-mail messages must be grammatically correct, and be sure to use a spell checker. But remember that certain words may be spelled correctly but used incorrectly, so the spell checker might not catch your usage errors.

Because it's so easy and fast, people tend to get careless or too casual with e-mail. To enhance your professional appearance, make your messages intelligent and as formal as the situation calls for. Guidelines for thoughtful e-mail communication are known as "netiquette." Here are some suggestions:

- Use short paragraphs, so readers won't have to scroll down through more than one screen to read them.

- Because e-mail isn't private, be prudent and don't express anything you wouldn't want to become public. And remember, once you send it, you can't retrieve it.

- Be careful of how you phrase your messages. Anger, sarcasm, and humor may be misunderstood when they are written rather than spoken. And don't use all caps—IT LOOKS AS THOUGH YOU ARE ANGRY AND SHOUTING AT THE RECIPIENT.

- Learn how to attach files so that the recipient can read them. If you can't find out what format works best, send the file as part of the message. If you forward files that you've received from someone else, be sure to delete unrelated material, also called "bloat."

- Resist "spamming"—or sending advertising messages to people you don't already have a relationship with. People resent it and react unfavorably.

Even if you don't use a computer, or if you are traveling without one, you can use a new product called PocketMail. A sending/receiving keyboard with a readout enables you to compose your e-mail message and send it via toll-free phone lines. You can also receive e-mail the same way. The device costs less than $140 and the monthly telephone service is about $10.

Tip 45

Choose your mailing and shipping methods wisely

Doing business by mail order is one of the ways that a home-based business, no matter where it may be located, can compete with bigger merchandisers. Mail and package-delivery services have become extremely competitive. Compare the rates offered by the U.S. Postal Service (USPS) with those offered by United Parcel Service (UPS) and Federal Express (FedEx) to make sure that you are handling your mailing and shipping in the most efficient and economical way.

For example, current rates for sending a two-pound package via USPS Priority Mail start at $3.20 (with 35¢ extra for delivery confirmation) compared with $7.50 to $11.00 for FedEx 2Day and $7.50 to $11.50 for UPS 2nd Day. Priority Mail's average delivery takes two to three days.

Seminars are offered frequently by the USPS that acquaint small-business owners with the range of its services. Access the USPS Web site, www.usps.gov, for postage calculations and the latest addressing information. USPS Publication 2, *Packaging for Mailing*, and Publication 227, *Preparing Packages for Mailing*, contain more tips and are available free from your post office.

Tip 46

Avoid making trips to the post office

Buy stamps by phone (1-800-STAMP24), by mail, or from postal self-service vending machines. Or use a postage meter, although you must periodically take it to the post office for postage to be added.

It's now possible to buy postage software for your computer. Here's how one of the Internet postage systems, E-stamp, works: A scale hooks into your PC, and your mail is weighed and the appropriate postage generated onto a sticker, which you apply like a stamp. The provider charges a $9 monthly fee for the service, and you pay for it and your postage by credit card. At this writing, E-stamp was available for $49.99, and included $50 worth of free postage. One of the supplier's selling points is that the software tracks your postage expenditures for a record of this business expense.

Official Internet postage providers are ClickStamp Plus and ClickStamp Online; E-stamp Internet Postage and E-stamp Online; PC Stamp; Postage Plus; Simply Postage, and Stamps.com Internet Postage. Your computer can also generate mailing labels.

The USPS will deliver boxes and envelopes for priority mail shipping right to your door. Another convenient option is to set up an account with UPS or FedEx so packages can be picked up at your home. This might require a monthly minimum-volume usage amount.

Tip 47

Use an Associated Mail and Parcel Center (AMPC)

Another alternative to the post office is a commercial mailbox service, or AMPC, such as Mailboxes Etc. A recently established USPS rule forbids the use of a suite number or anything else in an AMPC address that would suggest that it is the actual physical location of a business, rather than a mail drop. The reasons for this rule are that people might be misled and box holders might engage in mail fraud—although their actual addresses must be on file, which makes fraudulent practices more difficult to get away with. Remember that if your mail fails to reach your mail center—which is considered the addressee—it is returned to the sender, not forwarded to your home.

One of the advantages of a mail service center is that you can ask advice about the best way to ship packages—for example, USPS, UPS, or FedEx—and they will help you choose the best, fastest, or safest. Although their box rentals cost more than the USPS, the range of services offered may make them a good solution for your business mailing needs.

Tip 48

Learn your local zoning laws

"Location, location, location." You've heard that phrase countless times in discussions about real estate, but it is even more critical when you are talking about a home-based business. Legal problems can and do frequently arise, depending on the location of the business and the type of business. One of the chief concerns of local government is whether a home-based business will increase traffic, noise, or noxious fumes that are going to cause local residents to complain to the authorities. Parking is another concern. Our city, for example—Thousand Oaks, California—doesn't regulate how many vehicles can be parked at a single residence, but it does not permit you to park on your driveway for more than thirty consecutive days. It also prohibits the parking of any vehicle in a yard area. This prohibition varies depending on the zoning of the property.

Thousand Oaks does permit businesses to be conducted from homes, but the city issues both a business license and a home occupation permit giving the home-based business permission to operate. Applicants have to describe the business and state what kind of materials they will use and whether the business will have employees. Signs advertising your business can be a problem if you put up a sign that is larger than the city allows or that has questionable content (for instance, a sign advertising fortune telling, which is frequently regulated).

Zoning consists of four main categories: agricultural, commercial, residential, and industrial. These categories are frequently broken down into subcategories, such as light industrial or single-family residential. There are different covenants (promises) and restrictions for home-based businesses. Covenants are promises that you, the homeowner, agreed to abide by when you purchased the property.

Depending on the type of business you conduct, logic will help a great deal in deciding how you can expand. Breeding potbellied pigs in a small Midwest town might be acceptable, but you will probably run into problems if you try it in a large metropolitan area such as New York City. Most zoning issues are not really a problem if you live in a rural environment where neighbors are not close by.

The best place to look for zoning information, if you live in a city, is city hall. City officials are usually very helpful in answering your questions about running a business since, if you are successful, your tax money will be flowing into the city coffers. Most city halls have a large zoning map with the different designations posted, and it is simply a matter of finding your location. If you live in an unincorporated area, the county officials will also have zoning maps for you to check out.

After you find out the zoning for your home, the next step is to find out what restrictions, if any, apply. Keep in mind that there are federal, state, county, and city statutes that might affect what you can do, as well as covenants and restrictions (CC&Rs) if you live in a tract home or sub-division. Federal laws dictate what you can manufacture in your home. If you want further information regarding federal laws, you can check the Code of Federal Regulations at your local library or check it out on the U.S. government Web site: www.accessgpo.gov/nara/cfr/index.html.

Even if you have jumped through all the hoops with the local authorities, there are still the neighbors to consider. Some neighborhoods have restrictions on remodeling, so if you are thinking of expanding your home to accommodate your growing business, you may need approval of your blueprints. A business that has clients coming to the house in the early morning hours might upset a neighbor who works nights and sleeps during the day. A nice friendly chat about your plans might just prevent that certain neighbor from complaining about your business plans. If you are running a home business that requires customers to park their cars on your street, talk to the neighbors and let them know that you will take care of any problems that might arise from a lack of parking spaces. Even if you are legally compliant, , a neighbor who doesn't like what you are doing can make your life miserable. Remember, being a good neighbor means communicating. Let your neighbors know what your plans are, and listen to their concerns.

Tip 49

Carry adequate liability insurance coverage

Other important considerations when running a home-based business are property and liability insurance. Here are some questions that you should consider when reviewing your insurance coverage:

- *To what extent are clients physically present on your property?* If they come to you for services or to pick up merchandise, do they actually come into your home?

- *Are you in possession of property that actually belongs to your clients?* A good example of this type of business is repairing or restoring valuable jewelry or antiques. The old "what if" scenario comes into play here; suppose someone wanders into your workshop and damages the antique table you have just repaired.

- *Do you store your merchandise in a warehouse?* Keeping an inventory record forces you to keep track accurately in case of loss.

- *Would the loss or destruction of the merchandise or service you provide affect your clients' livelihood?* Is clients' property—such as financial records, databases, or seasonal merchandise—on your premises? What if someone wants to see what kind of neat games you have on your computer and accidentally deletes some irreplaceable client files? Another diabolical "what if" scenario could occur if a hacker stole data, including your client's, from your computer, and sold it to one of your client's competitors.

- *Do you use your car or truck for business purposes?* If you do, then make sure that you get the appropriate insurance for the vehicle.

- *Do you work at the client's site?* If so, you should probably consider some type of contractual liability insurance. In other words, check with the client and see what type of coverage they have. You might not need to purchase your own policy.

There are two insurance options for the owner of a home-based business. The homeowner's Class 2 policy is broader than a basic policy and usually will specify the business items covered. The homeowner's Class 3 policy offers the broadest coverage of the property and its contents. Usually, the Class 2 policy has an added endorsement from the insurance carrier to cover some aspects of the home-based business, while the Class 3 policy provides full coverage.

Limited liability has always been part of a homeowner's policy and has usually been enough. If a homeowner failed to perform a service as promised, then the client would simply take his business elsewhere. In our much more litigious society, however, not having enough property and liability insurance can be a disaster.

The key question that the home-based businessperson has to answer is whether or not she is really running a business. There are some fairly significant tax breaks for a true business. In order to take advantage of them, Pat Borowski of the National Association of Professional Agents says, "make sure your coverage protects the function, equipment, and location of the office and equipment."

Here's an example of the importance of having the right insurance coverage: A basic homeowner's policy will cover food spoilage due to a power outage and resultant loss of refrigeration. But if a homeowner makes a claim on his policy for the loss of twelve dozen custard pies and the insurance adjustor discovers during a routine investigation that the homeowner is actually running a catering business, the claim will more than likely be rejected.

It's not just an extra large claim that will be viewed suspiciously by the insurance company: A typical homeowner's policy, for example, provides only $2,500 in coverage for business equipment stored at your home. This amount is unlikely to cover the cost of all the business property. If a claim is made for a loss of equipment that is obviously designed for commercial use, then you have a problem.

Consider an endorsement to your existing homeowner's policy. For less than $20 a year, you can approximately double your standard policy limits from $2,500 to $5,000. Be aware that, generally, endorsements are available only for businesses that have $5,000 or less in annual receipts.

Because of the growth of home-based businesses, some insurance companies are creating special home-business insurance policies. The cost is about $200 a year, and this will insure your business property for $10,000. General liability coverage is included in the typical policy. These policies will also cover lost income and ongoing expenses, such as payroll, for up to one year if your business is unable to operate because of damage to your home. There is also limited coverage for loss of valuable business records.

Most homeowner's policies will cover the homeowner for defamation in a nonbusiness situation. If, for example, you announce to the world that your next-door neighbor is a criminal and the neighbor doesn't agree with your assessment and sues you for libel or slander (which are two subcategories under defamation), your insurance company will probably agree to defend you. However, if your home-based business entity makes some defamatory remarks about a competitor and the competitor sues you and the company, your homeowner's policy is not going to help you.

Malpractice insurance is another item to consider, depending on what type of business you have. It is commonly called "errors and omissions" insurance, or E&O. This type of insurance is something to consider if you work in a profession such as law or accounting.

Sometimes a company selling you a home-business policy will insist that you also purchase a homeowner's and auto policy from them. Whether you shop for insurance over the Internet or from an agent, make sure that you tell them that you have a home-based business and that you are interested in a package deal.

Tip 50

Shop for business insurance on the Internet

Use the Internet to shop for insurance of all sorts. Not to disparage our good friends who are insurance agents, but some of them will try to steer you into purchasing insurance from companies that give *them* the biggest commission, not necessarily companies that give you the best price. We are at the beginning of a revolution when it comes to insurance and other services of this nature. The financial-services firm Morgan Stanley estimates that 15 percent of all auto insurance will be purchased on the Internet by the year 2003.

There are numerous Web sites dealing with insurance of all sorts, and you can get a list of them by using any large search engine on the Internet. Right now, less than 1 percent of insurance transactions are started online, but consumers are rapidly changing the way they shop for insurance by obtaining quotes and comparing services using Web sites. By comparing prices on the Internet, you can eliminate the agent or middleman and pocket the difference yourself.

Tip 51

Pay for worker's compensation insurance

What if you have part-time or seasonal workers in your home-based business? Suppose you put together dried-flower arrangements, and you occasionally have someone come in to help with the arranging. If so, you must pay for worker's compensation insurance. This is also necessary if you have someone come into your home to take care of your child while you attend to the business. By the way, don't think for a minute that you can rely on written waivers signed by people who are working at your home. If a court finds that a person working for you is an employee rather than an independent contractor, the waiver is worth nothing and you could end up paying for this person's medical coverage for the rest of his life.

There are a number of factors that the courts look to to determine whether a person is an employee or an independent contractor. In an employment relationship, you have the right to control and direct the activities of your employee and the manner and method in which her work is performed, whether or not that right is actually exercised. But there is a pretty safe way to make your own determination: If you are not sure whether the person is an independent contractor or an employee, the courts will probably conclude that she is an employee.

Tip 52

Compare medical insurance

The new tax laws have made it easier on the self-employed to have medical insurance and to actually be able to take a tax deduction. As of the year 2000, you can deduct 50 percent of the cost of your health insurance premiums. This figure will gradually increase until the year 2007, when you will be able to deduct 100 percent of your premiums.

Do some checking on the Internet to get a feel for what is offered and how much it will cost. Of course, medical insurance will vary greatly depending on the size of your family and the state of your health. You will have to make some decisions as to whether or not you will join a health maintenance organization (HMO) or a preferred provider organization (PPO). Frequently, it is easier and cheaper to get insurance if you are a member of a group such as a professional or alumni association.

HMOs provide, or ensure delivery of, health care in a certain geographic area. In exchange for a fixed premium, they offer an agreed-on set of basic and supplemental services to a voluntarily enrolled group of people. Generally, there are either no deductibles or minimal copayments. However, there has been much recent controversy about HMO's quality of service, such as decisions about whether certain medical conditions are deserving of high-cost referrals that will cost the HMO more money.

PPOs generally consist of groups of hospitals and providers that contract with employers, insurers, and third-party administrators to provide health-care services to covered persons and to accept negotiated fees as payment. The cost to the consumer for a PPO is generally higher than for an HMO, but lower than a fee-for-service program, which is the traditional form of medical treatment in the United States. Your insurance carrier pays the physician the reasonable and customary fee, and you are responsible for the balance if the physician charges more.

Medical savings accounts (MSAs) are a relatively new scheme to pay for medical expenses, including health-plan deductibles. Self-employed individuals or their spouses are eligible to establish an MSA when they carry high-deductible health-care coverage and no other insurance, with some exceptions. Contributions to MSAs are deductible from your gross earnings for state and federal tax purposes, and can be used tax-free for all qualified medical expenses. And, similar to an individual retirement account (IRA), any balance you don't spend can be rolled over year-to-year tax free while earning interest. A limited number of MSAs have been made available as part of a nationwide federal pilot program. Consult your insurance agent and tax adviser, or refer to Internal Revenue Service Publication 1999 Form 5498-MSA.

Tip 53

Protect yourself with disability insurance

Disability insurance is a real *must* for the home-based business owner. This type of insurance is easily available and not costly. Disability insurance protects an individual against loss of income that can arise from a serious injury or illness. It doesn't matter if the injury is considered industrial (job-related) or not. Worker's compensation insurance is required in all states and covers people only for injuries that arise out of or during the course of employment. Worker's compensation insurance typically doesn't pay as high a benefit as disability insurance.

Believe it or not, disability insurance is more valuable to a young person than group life insurance, since it is more likely that a young individual will be disabled than die prematurely. One survey done by the National Association of Insurance Commissioners found that a thirty-five-year-old man has a 19 percent chance of becoming disabled for ninety days before he reaches age sixty-five. Women are in an even worse position; a thirty-five-year-old woman has a 29 percent chance of a ninety-day period of disability before she turns sixty-five.

Now compare the above figures with the chances of dying: A man has only a 0.2 percent chance of dying at the age of thirty-five. For women, the numbers are slightly lower, since women live longer than men. It may be a little misleading to compare the two numbers, since disability looks for the risk over many years and the death statistics consider the risk of dying for only one year. But even taking that into account, disability is a much larger threat.

Another factor to consider in deciding whether to purchase disability insurance is that there are many diseases that once were fatal but now are easily survivable because of our huge advances in medical treatment. However, many of these survivors live with conditions that do not permit them to work for a living. A common observation among actuaries is that mortality is down, but morbidity is up. In other words, illness and injury doesn't kill young people anymore; it just disables them for long periods of time.

One of the first things to look for in a disability insurance policy is that it cover both short-term and long-term disability. Short-term refers to up to six months, and long-term disability takes over at that point. Most experts recommend that long-term disability insurance cover the person for at least two years, if not more. Of course, the longer the period that benefits are paid, the higher the premium will be. Benefits should equal about 60 percent of the worker's gross income; for example, a person with a gross income of $100,000 should have benefits paying $60,000. Insurance companies will not issue policies for 100 percent of your income, since it would discourage you from going back to work. Another thing to look for is disability insurance that defines disability as being disabled in "one's own occupation." In other words, the disabled person is unable to engage in his or her own particular occupation. Watch out for policies that define "disabled" to mean that the person is unable to engage in *any* occupation for which they are reasonably suited by training, education, or experience. It would be very difficult to collect on this policy and the insurance companies know it.

There are other insurance policies that refuse to pay if the person is disabled because of stress or soft-tissue injures that are difficult to confirm. If you claim that you have a bad back or carpal-tunnel syndrome, these policies are not going to help.

Naturally, a good policy such as one that defines disability to mean "in one's own occupation" costs more, and it's worth it. If you, the injured worker, have paid the premium, you don't pay income tax on the benefits. In a high tax bracket, it's almost like getting your full salary!

Tip 54

Safeguard your independent-contractor status

There are a number of factors to look at when determining whether an individual is an employee or an independent contractor (IC). As an IC, you are not paid any benefits by the employer. As an employee, you will not be able to take any of the write-offs that are available to ICs. It can be costly if the IRS audits you and finds out that you were really an employee, not an IC. The company that is now considered to be your employer will not be happy, since they will be liable for not having taken deductions from the paychecks they gave you. Remember, the IRS prefers that companies make deductions, since the chance of fraud is not as great as with a self-employed individual who might be tempted to not declare the check as income.

Tip 55

Get a sales-tax exemption

Buy wholesale; otherwise you're paying sales tax twice. Get a vendor's license or a tax ID number, which makes you eligible to avoid paying sales tax on the items you use to produce your product. Depending on the supplier, you may be required to fill out an exemption certificate (a form, usually supplied by the state, that provides information about the purchaser), which the supplier will keep on file. However, you might have to fill out a certificate every time you make a purchase, so it's a good practice to have your license or tax ID number with you at all times.

Typically, companies will not give you a super deal just because you have a sales-tax exemption, but it may give you a chance to haggle with the supplier and build a relationship. Find out from the supplier if there are volume discounts available. A lot of suppliers will require you to buy amounts that the usual consumer would not be interested in. (We don't mean members-only discount stores such as Costco, although you can frequently get some good deals at such places.) A good example is in the food business, where there is a considerable price break if you buy a 50-pound drum of dry mustard, rather than those little 2-ounce jars that you find in the supermarkets. Unfortunately, most wholesalers have minimum-order amounts. Building-supply stores such as Home Depot and Lowe's will consider discounts for volume purchases, and so will office-supply stores such as Staples and Office Depot. However, it's necessary to talk to the manager of the store in order to secure a deal.

Tip 56

Sign written contracts with your customers

A contract doesn't have to be in legalese, but it does have to spell out its essential terms. A letter of agreement simply detailing what is being purchased, along with quantity, price, and delivery terms, is the normal procedure that small businesses use to conduct their business. A business invoice has all the important information on it and confirms the terms of the contract. The software programs Quicken and Microsoft Money provide invoices that are very useful.

Frequently, business relationships that are ongoing rely on verbal contracts between the two parties. However, if you are dealing with someone you don't know or with a large corporation, it's much smarter to put an agreement in writing. Make sure that if you have some questions about the terms you consult your lawyer to determine that the contract says what you think it says.

Tip 57

Patent your unique invention

Have you come up with a great idea that is going to make you the next Bill Gates? Protect this unique idea by applying for a patent. There are hundreds of thousands of inventors and innovators who file each year for protection under U.S. patent laws.

Patents protect an inventor's discoveries and are granted in three categories: utility, design, and plant. The law doesn't permit you to get a patent on a mere idea, suggestion, or method of doing business.

Utility is the broadest category of patents. To earn a utility patent, an invention must be useful and fit into at least one of five subcategories: a process, a machine, a manufacture, a composition of matter, or an improvement of an existing idea that falls into one of these categories. Often an invention will fall into more than one category. Computer software, for example, can be described as both a process (the steps it takes to make a computer operate) and a machine (an instrument that carries information from an input device to an output device).

Design patents are granted for the invention of designs that are innovative, nonfunctional, and part of a functional manufactured article. For example, a new shape for a car fender or flashlight that doesn't improve overall functionality would qualify.

Plant patents are just what their name implies. Examples of this would be a new color of climbing rose or a new variety of apple.

Utility and plant patents are granted for twenty-year periods from the date of application, whereas design patents are granted for fourteen years.

Obtaining a patent can be a long and tedious process. The application involves more than just filling out a simple form. The application must be written in great detail and include drawings of the work. The patent must enable someone skilled in the particular area to reproduce the invention without undue experimentation. It is also necessary to include one or more "claims" that describe the specific aspects of the invention that warrant the issue of a patent. Effective composition of this claim is critical. The claim has to refer to devices currently being used or likely to be used in the not-too-distant future.

If you are interested in obtaining a patent, retain a registered patent attorney to prepare your application. Patent attorneys are listed in the Yellow Pages of your local phone directory. The cost of such a service depends on how complex the idea is, since the attorney will bill you by the hour.

Be careful to whom you talk about your invention, since you have no protection for your idea until the application is filed. However, under U.S. patent laws, you have a one-year grace period in advance of your application. During that time, you can disclose or commercialize your invention in any way. However, if you describe your work in a publication or commercialize it at any time beyond that year and before applying for a patent, your application can be denied.

Most inventors don't develop or manufacture their patented work themselves, since that requires a considerable monetary investment that is beyond the means of the typical inventor. The inventor usually makes arrangements with an existing company to do it all for him. The inventor licenses the developer to exploit the invention in return for paying royalties to the inventor.

Tip 58

Trademark your product

Trademarks protect good will that is created when customers associate a company's name—or other indicator of source, origin, or sponsorship—with a product or service. These indicators can be things like product packaging, a likeness, or even a scent.

Trademark law is based on the concept of first usage. In other words, you don't have to register a trademark to establish rights to it. You can create a "common law" right simply by using it, thus establishing prior use. These trademark rights can last indefinitely if you continue to use the mark to identify your goods or services.

Registration does have its advantages. Once your mark is registered with the U.S. Patent and Trademark Office, you can use your trademark and the symbol ^{TM} with your product or service. Registration does not guarantee that no one else will try to use your trademark, but it gives you credibility if someone uses it and claims prior use.

Do a trademark search first! It can save you a lot of problems down the road if you know in advance that someone has already registered the trademark. The one who used it first, and registered it, wins. There are some very useful software programs available for a few hundred dollars that will permit you to perform a search yourself via the Internet. There are also professional search agencies that will perform a search for a fee, typically several hundred dollars, which would be the preferred method if you have only a single trademark in which you are interested.

Tip 59

Copyright your book

A copyright protects authors and artists from the unfair use of their original work "fixed" in a "tangible" medium. The word "fixed" is used to prevent people from trying to copyright an idea that is not acted upon. "Tangible" means things like books, recordings, or even computer programs.

Copyright law applies to all types of original expression, including literature, sculpture, choreography, CD-ROMs, video games, and even flow charts. Publication is not required for protection. The key to understanding copyright law is to understand the difference between an idea and the expression of an idea. Copyright applies only to a particular expression, not the ideas or facts underlying it. You can copyright a song about a romance in the big city, but you can't copyright the underlying idea of having a love affair in the big city.

There are three criteria that must be met in order to be protected by a copyright:

1. It must be original, not copied.

2. It must be fixed in a tangible medium as discussed above.

3. It has to have at least some creativity; that is, it must be produced by an exercise of human intellect.

A work created on or after January 1, 1978, will be automatically protected for the duration of its author's life plus an additional seventy years after the author's death. If a work is authored jointly by two or more people not working for hire, then the term of the copyright will last for 70 years after the last surviving author's death. If the work was made for hire, anonymously, then the duration of the copyright is extended to 95 years from publication or 120 years from its creation, whichever is shorter. Remember, you don't legally have to register your trademark, but you must register before you sue someone for copyright infringement.

For more information, write to the following address:

> Publications Section LM-455
> U.S. Copyright Office
> Library of Congress
> Washington, DC 20559
> (202) 287-9100
> Web site: http://www.loc.gov/copyright/

Tip 60

Save for your retirement *before* paying income tax

Below are several ways for the home-based business owner to prepare for retirement.

A simple IRA is an individual retirement account that permits individuals to save from $2,000 to $6,000 of pretax income every year, and defer taxation on that money until it is withdrawn. It works fine for individuals, although it is not as versatile as a profit-sharing plan. Its maintenance costs are laughably low: $10 a year per participant. The great thing about these plans is that there are no tax-filing requirements.

A SEP-IRA is a simplified employee pension and is available to businesses of any size, including sole proprietorships. The plan is simple and easy to administer. On top of that, contributions are voluntary. If a contribution is made, however, it must be the same percentage for each eligible employee. The SEP is ideal for companies with one or two employees, because there are no plan administration fees or IRS filings, and employees are immediately vested 100 percent.

Keogh plans were created to provide a tax-sheltered retirement option for self-employed taxpayers. You are eligible to establish a Keogh plan if you own a business or part of a business that is not incorporated. The business must be operating as a sole proprietorship, a partnership, or a limited liability company. You have to actually perform personal services for the company; passive investment is not enough. Keogh plans now are very similar to retirement plans for corporations. Like the 401(k) plan, eligible employees are anyone age twenty-one or older with 1,000 hours of service. Unfortunately, Keogh plans are every bit as complex as the plans for corporations. Because of this, we strongly suggest that you consult with a tax adviser specializing in this area.

Tip 61

Deal with your customers on a personal level

Even in this age of technological gadgets such as answering machines and voice mail, small businesspeople are in an excellent position to personalize customer contacts, because they often do business one-on-one. Make every effort to respond to customer telephone calls within twenty-four hours. If they're unhappy, show your concern. Make follow-up calls or send letters to make sure they are satisfied with the product or service you provided.

Of course, there will be times when transactions don't go as smoothly as they should, but if your clients feel that you really care about their satisfaction, they will be willing to put up with some occasional inconvenience. It doesn't cost you anything to smooth a few ruffled feathers in the interest of retaining customers.

You can offer expedited delivery or shipping, discounts, or other special payment considerations. If you have a deadline and don't think you can meet it, let your customer know as soon as possible that you're experiencing difficulties, and when you expect to deliver. Keep the lines of communication open to avoid misunderstandings and customer disappointment. According to the Customer Service Institute, 65 percent of a company's business comes from existing customers, and it costs five times as much to attract a new customer as to keep an existing one satisfied. Studies by the Technical Assistance Research Programs Institute found that 91 percent of unhappy customers said they'd never buy again from a company that has displeased them; and furthermore, they would voice their dissatisfaction to at least seven other people. Remember that word of mouth in the form of referrals by satisfied customers is the least expensive and most effective public-relations asset we have.

If customers didn't enjoy doing business face-to-face with someone they know and trust, we'd all be buying everything from catalogs and vending machines. Even if you have a mail-order business, your telephone manner and personalized service can make a big difference. Many mail-order companies include personal messages from the owners in their catalogs, sometimes including staff photographs and stressing the person-to-person quality of their product or service. Make sure that people feel that there is a real, live person running your operation, someone they can rely on and to whom they can relate.

Today's customers demand more service, and are willing to pay a little extra for it. Small, home-based businesses can take advantage of this trend, because their products and services can be tailored to individual needs. Consumers want to know who creates the products they buy and where to turn for advice and adjustment when they're needed. They're tired of getting lip service instead of customer service from the representatives of large corporations that seem to put profits, and not consumers, first.

Tip 62

Don't be nearsighted—set long-range goals

Sit down and make long-term plans. You probably started out with a pretty good blueprint when you launched your business, but you need to pay constant attention to the adjustments that must be made as you progress.

Hugh Scott's company, Scott Cards, designed, printed, and sold its own cards, and he also designed cards for Recycled Paper Greetings. When the salesman who was responsible for selling and delivering Scott Cards to retail stores quit, Hugh decided it would be a lot less trouble to just sell his designs and not be involved in manufacturing and marketing them. Nowadays, he uses his computer to generate the graphics for his designs. His current goal is to create one card every day to submit to Recycled Paper Greetings for consideration.

Like Hugh, all of us should set goals. Make it a point to set aside some time to decide what you need to accomplish this week, this month, this quarter, this year, and five years from now. Even if these objectives aren't set in stone, thinking ahead will help you stay focused. Sometimes we become so engrossed in the immediate demands of running a business that we aren't thinking about the future. When the current job is finished, another one must take its place.

At the conclusion of a sale or project, make it clear that you are interested in the client's future business. Instead of just a thank-you for the patronage, suggest a debriefing to analyze the completed transaction and how the next project could be improved. You might prepare a summary of how the work was accomplished and make suggestions for even better results next time. This will help to position you for further involvement. At the very least, express an interest in bidding on future work. Then make notes to remind yourself to keep in touch and contact the client when the appropriate time approaches.

Tip **63**

Develop a marketing plan

Consider the four basic aspects of marketing, which the Small Business Administration refers to as the "4 P's."

- *Product:* The item or service you sell.

- *Price:* The amount you charge for your product or service.

- *Promote:* The ways you inform your market as to who, what, and where you are.

- *Provide:* The channels you use to take the product to the customer.

You may need to develop a separate marketing plan for each service or each single item that you manufacture and/or sell. On the other hand, perhaps you can group your services or products together and handle the marketing of all of them in the same way. Your plan doesn't have to be a formal written document, unless you are submitting it to a lending source from which you hope to obtain a loan. But putting it in writing might help you to do a more thorough job of thinking your plan through.

You will have to determine which products or services should be emphasized for primary marketing efforts, and which ones can be considered secondary. In the case of a makeup consultant who sells cosmetics, for example, the consulting service is the primary product, and the cosmetics are a secondary or ancillary product.

Next, determine the prices you will need to charge—wholesale or retail (depending on who you'll be selling to)—taking into account the actual cost of production plus a margin for profit. Compare this with the prices of similar services or products in your marketplace to make sure you are competitive.

Now you must evaluate the best ways to promote your product. First, you need to have a clear idea of just who and where your market is. Then decide how best to reach those potential buyers. This might be via word of mouth and referrals, advertising in various media, participating in trade shows, giving out free samples, or doing *pro bono* work (where you contribute your service to a nonprofit organization at no cost for the purpose of gaining exposure and good will).

Hopefully, the orders will come rolling in, and your only other problem will be supplying those hordes of buyers demanding what you have to offer! Your channels of distribution are an important part of your marketing plan, because your ultimate success or failure depends on delivering your product to your customers.

Tip 64

Conduct ongoing market research

Over time, you may discover that your potential customer base has changed. Look for new audiences to target. Your product may have special appeal to a particular market segment, such as new-home purchasers, pet owners, or working women. It may be more profitable to concentrate on a tight geographic area, to minimize travel or shipping expenses.

You might want to conduct simple surveys by mail or phone to discover who your potential customers really are. Unfortunately, mail surveys have a low response rate, unless there are high incentives, such as prizes or free samples to the first one hundred respondents. A self-addressed stamped envelope (SASE) or reply card must be included with the questionnaire. This type of survey tends to be filled out more often by retirees, rather than younger working people, and this may skew your results away from your target audience.

The following customer survey, which could be used as a mail questionnaire or a phone survey of past customers, was developed by the Small Business Administration:

1. How did you first hear about our product/service?

2. Have you seen any of our advertising? If so, where?

3. What do you like best/find most useful about our product/service?

4. How could our product/service be improved?

5. What other products/services would you like us to offer?

6. What was the single most compelling reason for choosing our product/service?

7. What other reasons were important?

8. What friends, family members, or colleagues, if any, influenced your buying decision?

9. What newspapers and magazines do you read regularly?

10. Which radio and television stations do you tune in most frequently?

11. Please indicate your age and sex:
    18–34   35–49   50–65   66 +
    Male   Female

12. Please indicate your annual household income:
    Under $15,000 $16–24,000 $25–49,000 $50–100,000 $100,000+

    (For business customers, modify #11 to inquire about the size of the company, such as number of employees. Modify #12 to ask for annual sales volume.)

In-person and telephone surveys are more expensive and time-consuming, but they usually generate higher response rates. You could do this kind of survey yourself, but respondents tend to tell you what they think you want to hear, so it's usually better to have someone else do it for you. If you don't want to hire a market-research firm, at least have the person doing the interviewing give the impression that they are not part of your company, but rather a disinterested and objective third party.

Another idea is to evaluate each encounter with customers to monitor the quality of your products and/or services. Use a short questionnaire to be mailed back to you as a follow-up to each sale or service call. Make sure each question concerns only one issue; "Was the person you dealt with prompt and courteous?" is two questions. Try to avoid "yes or no" questions and offer check-off ratings ("On a scale of 1 to 10, . . .") in no more than four questions, ensuring that customers are putting their ideas into short answers more often than mechanically checking boxes.

When your questionnaires have been returned or interviews completed, you can analyze the results to better comprehend:

- what your company's strong and weak points are;

- whether customers are responding to your advertising, what advertising is most effective, and what could be more effective;

- what product benefits should be stressed in your advertising; and

- the demographic makeup of your market. Who are they, and can they afford your product or service?

If the stakes are high enough and you are thinking of making a huge investment in a new product, you may want to hire a professional research firm to conduct focus groups or surveys for you. But be prepared to pay a high price for such a service. Focus groups often cost as much as $1,000 each, and one group is not a sufficient sample.

Read the local papers to find out what trends are taking shape in your area. Keep your eyes and ears open. For example, it might help to visit neighborhood stores to see what people are buying and what your competition is offering. If you offer a service, pose as a potential customer (or have a friend or family member do this) to comparison-shop the competition. Study advertising, business, and trade publications to get an idea of the pricing of goods and services similar to yours.

Create a profile of your best customer. Is it someone seeking prestige, comfort, convenience, security, or a bargain? What will make this person want to buy from you rather than your competitors? If your product is similar to others, what little "something extra" can you offer in the way of customer service that will tip the scales in your favor? Try to think like a buyer.

Find out what newspapers or magazines your customers read, and what television or radio programs they watch and listen to. This will give you some idea of what kind of media and advertising they will be most likely to respond to.

Tip 65

If you have a service business, sell associated products

A cleaning service might sell maintenance products that you have tried and found useful. Kathie Jo Kadziauskas owns Crime Scene Steam and Clean, certainly a niche-market business. Kathie is hired by families and insurance companies to clean homes and other locations where deaths or injuries have occurred. She is also a dealer for an antiodor product, ExStink, which she uses in her business and has found to be extremely effective.

Pet groomers frequently sell brushes, combs, clippers, and soaps. Other possibilities for pet-care providers would be dog food, treats, beds, leashes, and other dog and cat needs.

Someone offering personal care—massage, beauty treatments, manicures, or hair care—would certainly profit from selling a line of associated products. In many cases, co-op advertising funds are available from the manufacturer.

Many of the party-plan merchandisers combine a social or craft activity with selling the products needed. At parties given by the company Pampered Chef, attendees are shown how to create food items, and they can purchase gadgets, tools, and some ingredients needed to prepare the dishes at home. The company Creative Memories shows crafters how to assemble keepsake albums and sells the supplies. Ceramics workshops market greenware and glazes to the students who come to learn how to finish their own pieces.

If you teach adult-education classes, your students pay a fee for the class, plus a materials fee for any handouts and items needed. For a cooking class, the materials fee covers the food prepared and the recipe handouts. The teacher may endorse a particular line of knives and sell them; cookbooks also are logical items to sell at cooking classes.

Tip 66

Be a smart buyer

Michael and Jennifer Whitaker of Spinning Jenny advise, "It's not how much you sell an item for; it's what you pay for it in the first place." Think about it. Your selling price will be determined in part by the going rate for similar goods, and what people are willing to pay for an item. But the lower the wholesale price you pay, the greater your margin of profit.

If you can buy enough at one time to take a quantity discount or take advantage of some other special price breaks, you will maximize your buying power and your markup. Of course, you will have to manage your cash flow so that you have money available to make timely purchases. Many of us practice this kind of buying on a small scale by shopping at post-holiday sales or targeting seasonal and model-year closeouts, such as buying patio furniture at the end of the summer.

One of the drawbacks to this type of buying is that you have to carry the inventory of the goods if you stock up in large quantities, unless you can arrange to take delivery at a later date. You may not have adequate storage space, or may have to rent it, which might eliminate the financial advantage of buying in bulk.

Successful antiques dealers are quite good at spotting the choice buys at estate sales and other sources for vintage items. Frequently, sellers don't realize the value of what they have, but they may become wary if the dealer singles out a few pieces and inquires how much the seller will take for them. Rather than drawing attention to the best items, the dealer may offer to buy the whole houseful of furniture and other goods for a flat price. The profit on the most valuable pieces will compensate for the low prices the dealer will charge for the other, less desirable goods.

Tip 67

Price for profitability

The pricing strategy used by the majority of small businesses is cost-based pricing, which is determined by adding a fixed amount or percentage to your unit cost, customarily two times the cost. But demand-oriented pricing, which is designed to reflect the buyers' level of interest, and competition-oriented pricing, which is geared to the marketplace, are sometimes more profitable. These tactics allow pricing flexibility so that you can respond to changes in demand or competitors' prices. Particularly if you offer a range of products or services, you can use a combination of pricing strategies to maximize the profits from each.

Donald Tisdale, a real-estate investor, explains demand-oriented pricing with the following example: If you have rental property, the price should be just high enough that tenants occasionally move out because they don't want to pay that much. Keeping rents low so tenants won't move elsewhere means you aren't charging enough. And of course, you should also base the rent on what similar units in your area rent for—that's competition-oriented pricing.

However, keeping prices low can increase your market share. This means that even if your markup per item isn't large, you will make more sales and thereby increase your profits. But bear in mind that you might not be equipped to handle high demand for low-priced merchandise.

Smart shoppers believe they get what they pay for. Consumers expect to pay low prices for common or ordinary goods, but the same buyers are willing to pay a premium for what they perceive as high-end merchandise. Particularly in the case of small businesses, high-end or handmade merchandise or unique products or services will be likely to bring higher prices.

Estimate the price your customers will be willing to pay, based on demand and competition, taking into account psychological and motivational factors such as image, prestige, novelty, and impulse buying. A recent marketing phenomenon is limited-edition collectibles, which can be anything from ceramic plates to Christmas ornaments. Who could have predicted the popularity of Beanie Babies? Collectors will pay high prices to add certain items to their collections. Others buy for investment because they believe prices will eventually rise; however, antiques investors advise buying only what you like, because there's really no way to predict future trends.

Charge enough so that as you grow, you won't have to boost prices too much. It's tempting when you first market a product to keep the price low enough to attract the maximum number of buyers. But if you don't factor in possible fluctuations in the prices you pay for raw materials or wholesale merchandise, you might be forced to frequently raise your prices, and this is discouraging to your clientele. Try to set your original price high enough to maintain over the long term, even if it's just an educated guess.

Under certain conditions, however, you might want to lower prices. If your merchandise isn't moving fast enough, or your competitors are out-selling you because their prices are lower, you don't have much choice. Analyze the underlying factors—is the whole market area in decline, not just your own sales? Perhaps you want to increase your market share by undercutting the competition. Greater sales volume increases the rate of turnover, and this can increase profitability. If you offer a range of products, an occasional "2 for 1" sale or "loss leader" can stimulate overall sales, even though you don't make a profit on such promotions.

You can fend off the effect of a competitor's price cut by launching what Northwestern University marketing professor Philip Kotler calls a "nonprice counterattack." Introduce services or product improvements to emphasize the greater value you offer to buyers. You could also effectively lower prices by not charging for certain goods or services (such as shipping charges), or by offering a variety of discounts from your already-established unit price.

Tip 68

Project the proper image

If you don't want your clientele to know that you operate out of your home, you can give the appearance that your company is much bigger than it really is. Make sure your telephone-answering procedure and equipment compare well with the companies with which you compete, and that household noises—such as televisions, shouting children, and barking dogs—aren't overheard when you are on the phone.

On the other hand, if your customers are likely to appreciate that you are the owner of a home-based business, it might not hurt to have a somewhat more "folksy" approach. For example, if you deal in products for children, go ahead and let your precocious youngster record your voice-mail message. Just be sure that it's appropriate. Some home-business owners narrate their own radio commercials, or appear in television spots, and this can be very effective. But if you're not the best public speaker, this may not work for you. Stick to your own image and personality. Project the basics of who you are. Make sure that your advertising rings true.

If you're not a particularly good writer, get help. Use a grammar hotline, such as Linda M. De Vore's www.grammarnow.com, or get a ghost writer to do proposals and other formal messages for you. This goes for other written communication as well.

Stationery, labels, and packaging should reinforce the business name and its desired image. Always enclose something special with correspondence you send out: business cards, flyers about special offers, new price lists or catalogs, coupons, or gimmicks such as refrigerator magnets.

Tip 69

Choose an "umbrella" name and identity for your company

Keep in mind that your business will change over time, and names shouldn't be too specific or limited to allow for later expansion. At first, we considered Maxye's Mustard, but we finally chose Maxye's Pantry because it covers everything we can imagine marketing in the future, from the gourmet food items that we originally planned to other items and activities such as publishing and selling cookbooks, teaching cooking classes, and selling kitchen antiques.

A good name communicates an image to the product's target customers, motivates them to buy, is something they will remember, and is unique so that you can trademark it to prevent other businesses from using it. For example, "Kaleidosoap" is a play on words that covers a variety of handcrafted soaps, bath salts, and aromatherapy products made by the company. "Pup Start" is the business name used by a dog obedience trainer.

List several characteristics that make your company or product special. They can be descriptive of your product or the benefits to users of your service. Think about traits you want to convey, such as friendliness, expertise, or innovation. Look in your local Yellow Pages and search the Internet; don't choose a name that's similar to your competition's. For example, something that begins with "Computer" is probably a poor choice.

Be careful not to choose something that sounds off-color or translates into another language in a derogatory way. What is the vocabulary or language of your audience? Brainstorm with your friends and family, and spend several days imagining different applications for the names you're considering. Say them aloud to make sure they sound as good as they look on paper. A name should be easy to spell so people can jot it down, or find it in the phone book. If too cutesy and topical, a name might become dated over time.

Along with the sound of the name, you will want to build awareness with a distinctive identity or graphics that are clearly associated with your company. Does the name lend itself to a distinctive logo? Present your product or service consistently through your ads, mailers, packaging, and signage, so that people will recognize you instantly. Think of the trademarks that are familiar to all of us: McDonald's golden arches, Toys "Я" Us' distinctive spelling, and all of the Web site addresses that are actually company names, such as amazon.com.

Tip 70

Go after repeat business

What can you do to keep 'em coming back for more? Look for ways to offer more service, better merchandise, or some other value that makes you stand out from the crowd. Solving customers' problems is sometimes called "customer-centered" marketing. What's involved is not just profit margins, but increased gross revenues and market share.

According to the Customer Service Institute, 65 percent of a company's business comes from existing customers, and it costs five times as much to attract a new customer than to keep an existing one satisfied.

Let your customers know that you appreciate their choosing to do business with you. Encourage them to give you feedback and make suggestions that will help you succeed. Thank them and make after-the-sale calls to find out if your product or service met their expectations.

Send holiday greetings to let your customers know you are still there to fill their needs. Or, to avoid having your mailing lost in the avalanche at year-end holiday time, pick another time of year. A greeting at Thanksgiving, in advance of the usual holiday flurry, will certainly be noticed. You might recognize a client's birthday or the anniversary of the completion of the job you did for them, so spread out your greetings throughout the year accordingly. Or, choose Valentine's Day to show how much you care about your customers. Offer specials on the anniversary of the establishment of your company.

Offer a bonus for continued patronage, such as "A baker's dozen: thirteen months' service for the price of twelve months."

Set up a mailing list of previous customers and send out mailings or a periodic newsletter. It's low-cost advertising, and it keeps your name in front of people with whom you've already established a relationship. If you develop a new product or service, let them know about it. If they've already been satisfied doing business with you, they'll be more willing to consider your new idea.

Tip **71**

Get referrals
by offering incentives

Encourage your past customers to refer you or your products to friends and associates. Ask permission to list them as references when you are recruiting new customers. Give customers business cards that they can distribute for you. Offer discounts on future purchases, free products, or a month's free service for referrals they send to you. And whenever a new customer says "So-and-so recommended you," send a thank-you—and, if appropriate, a gift—to the customer who gave you the referral.

An article about our home-remodeling project was featured in the Real Estate section of the *Los Angeles Times*, and in it we complimented both the architect and the tile contractor for having done very good work. Neither one called to acknowledge the publicity, although months later we happened to meet the tile contractor, who said he'd had many sales leads as a result of the article. We never did hear from the architect, and we were disappointed that he didn't make an effort to thank us. We'll probably shop around for another architect next time.

Ask other home-business owners to refer clients to you, and offer to pay them a percentage or a finder's fee. A 10 or 20 percent fee is typical in many professions.

Tip **72**

Develop a mailing list and use it

Every contact, whether it results in a sale or not, is a name to add to your mailing list. Even if you only do one or two mailings a year, you will reach people who have already indicated an interest in your product or service. The more often they hear from you, the more likely they are to remember you when they need you or to talk with someone else who could become a new customer.

Steve and Maryellen Stofelano, owners of Mansion Hill Inn, in Albany, New York's inner-city Mansion District, were profiled in the Small Business Administration's Business Development/Success Series. Using a mailing list of diners who fill out comment cards that accompany dinner checks, the Stofelanos stay in touch with guests by sending notices of dinners or promotions like summertime room discounts for Albany residents. "Never forget," says Steve, "that your best customers are your existing customers."

Your mailings can be simple postcards, elaborate flyers, seasonal catalogs with order forms, or regular newsletters. Investigate the use of a bulk-mailing permit, which will save you postage costs if you presort your mail by zip code.

"Spamming," or sending unsolicited sales messages via e-mail, is frowned upon and resented by many recipients. If you do use this medium, offer an "unsubscribe" feature so that people can let you know they prefer to be dropped from your e-mail solicitation list.

Tip 73

Make new contacts every week

Set a goal to make a reasonable number of new contacts on a regular basis. You have to constantly widen your circle of potential customers and take a long-range view. Unfortunately, you will lose some customers—they may move out of the area, or their buying needs may change. Depending on your product or service, clients may not need to come back to you frequently, so you should constantly be looking for new ones. You also should seek a broad enough customer base so that the loss of one or two won't leave you without a livelihood.

Whether you make telephone calls, distribute flyers, send out press releases, or attend events where you can network, strive to introduce yourself to a specific number of new contacts every week, or at least every month. Your methods can be subtle: when you meet new people, find ways to ask about them, and casually volunteer information about yourself and your business. These contacts may not always become customers or clients themselves, but the idea is to get yourself and your product or service known to as many people as possible.

Tip 74

Speak for yourself

Volunteer to speak to professional or special-interest groups in your community to make them aware of what your business has to offer.

Participate in classes, seminars, and workshops where you can demonstrate your skills or showcase your merchandise. Workshops held at Small Business Development Centers are one possibility, and many civic organizations need speakers at meetings and luncheons. Make up a list of suggested topics that relate to your business, and contact the program directors or other appropriate club members.

Lou has taught seminars on labor law and workers' compensation issues for company personnel at workshops in our area. Employers are interested in avoiding worker complaints and possible lawsuits, so proper hiring and firing and other management practices and policies are understandably topics of interest.

Today's bookstores are more than just retail outlets; they provide entertainment and a relaxed atmosphere for browsing. Book signings are a way for authors to meet potential buyers of their books. Bookstore cafés feature local performance artists, who offer their recordings for sale.

Tip 75

Get involved in community affairs and charities

Join your local chamber of commerce, visitor and convention bureau, or other local trade association. Volunteer to teach a workshop at a senior citizens' center. Donate services or merchandise for charity auctions. If you're an entertainer, perform at a fund-raising event. Sponsor a local team, and supply uniforms with your company logo on them. These are all ways to spread the news about you and your business.

Steve and Maryellen Stofelano have taken on two tasks: renewing their neighborhood and promoting their Mansion Hill Inn. In the neighborhood, the couple's efforts at reviving their street have raised property values, won them a municipal award, and made Mansion Hill Inn a place where guests can feel safe. They've focused their marketing on their award-winning dining room. The Stofelanos serve only New York State wines, for example, which has brought them notice and acclaim. The couple also offers "Mansion Suppers" featuring the cuisines of their Polish, German, Italian, and African-American neighborhood.

"Designer houses" are showcases for the work of interior decorators, craftspeople, and landscape designers. An entire home is redecorated and opened for paid tours, usually as a fund-raiser for charity.

Offering *pro bono* services is another way to contribute to the community and bolster your public image. A public-relations consultant could donate creative talent to provide publicity for a nonprofit organization. Keep in mind that mileage and out-of-pocket expenses are tax-deductible, but time is not.

Tip 76

Join professional and trade organizations

The main purpose of belonging to a trade organization is having the opportunity to network with people in similar businesses and exchange ideas. Membership can also give the small-business owner the advantages of market research and other services that might be too expensive to take on oneself. Fringe benefits, such as group health or life insurance rates, are other reasons for belonging to a trade association.

Some of the national associations and organizations for home-based businesspeople are listed as follows:

American Association of Home-Based Businesses
P.O. Box 10023
Rockville, MD 20849
1-800-447-9710
Web site: www.aahbb.org

National Association of Home-Based Businesses
10451 Mill Run Circle
Owings Mills, MD 21117
(410) 581-0071
Web site: www.usahomebusiness.com

By networking with other home-based entrepreneurs (25 million in the United States and growing), you can learn from others' experience, and you can ask them to refer clients to you. Putting On the Ritz is a partnership comprising more than twenty-five small, diverse businesses specializing in photography, videography, catering, travel, beauty consulting, and entertainment. They work together to provide party services in their West Coast community. Members meet regularly and split advertising expenses.

Tip 77

Send out press kits and releases to get free publicity

Develop a press kit that explains who and what you are. This is a great way to get your message out to local and regional publications that can give you free publicity. Even national magazines run "New Product" sections—if the product featured gets a good response, they hope to gain a new advertiser as a result. Newspaper editors are most likely to publish material that needs a minimum of rewriting, so keep your press release basic and not too effusive.

Your press kit should include your company's name and location, a business card, and a press release with photos or a fact sheet. You can include a calendar of events you'll be participating in, a background sheet about who you are, your photograph, quotes and testimonials from satisfied customers, copies of published articles about you, and samples of your merchandise. Make it attractive and eye-catching. It's particularly convenient to use a folio cover that has a place to insert your business card; you might even think of having a business card that is actually notched to fit into a rotary card file, such as a Roladex.

Because your press release may be time-sensitive, be sure to date it, or indicate the optimum time for it to run. For instance, if you want pre-Christmas publicity, you might indicate "For November Release." Your telephone number, or that of a person acting as your public-relations contact, should appear prominently at the top. Offer to make the release available via e-mail or on a computer disk, to save the editor's time scanning or keyboarding.

The release itself should be short, simple, and concise. Use the Five-Ws-and-H technique: in the first paragraph, try to tell who, what, why, where, when, and how.

Jim Robertson, owner of Back 40 Landscaping, might send the following release:

> A free workshop, "Mulching for Lovelier Landscapes," will be presented by master gardener Jim Robertson at the Thousand Oaks Botanical Garden on Saturday, May 20, at 2 P.M.

The next paragraph should add information and answer questions that the reader may have:

> Robertson, proprietor of Back 40 Landscaping, will explain how mulching with organic material can improve soil and retain moisture in your yard, nurturing plants and protecting them from summer drought. Free mulch will be provided by the City of Thousand Oaks Department of Public Works. Attendees should bring two empty 30-gallon garbage cans. For more information, contact: (805) 555-1212.

Jim could enclose a glossy black-and-white photo of himself, with a caption that summarizes the press release pasted on the back of the photo. The caption could read:

> "Mulching for a Lovelier Landscape" will be the subject of a free workshop presented by Jim Robertson, of Back 40 Landscaping, at the Thousand Oaks Botanical Garden on Saturday, May 20, at 2 P.M.

This way, Jim has provided both a well-written news release and a captioned photo, which gives the newspaper editor the option of printing only the photograph and its caption or the entire release.

An alternative to sending out a press release is to write an article for a trade journal or other publication. You can then reprint and mail it to customers and prospects. This positions you as an expert in your field and is a particularly good way to promote a consulting business.

In many communities, you can arrange to have your own television or radio show on a public-service channel or station. Another idea is to make videos or take photos of completed projects to run on local TV channels. You can also show videos at trade fairs or to interested audiences, or put photos on your Web site.

Tip 78

Get product exposure at little or no cost

If your invention or product lends itself to photographic settings; display windows; or use as a movie, television, or advertising prop; offer it to companies that might be interested. One of Hugh Scott's greeting cards appeared in the opening credits of a major motion picture as a prop on the leading character's desk. Magazines use borrowed merchandise to dress interiors for photographic layouts, and they list sources so that readers know where the items can be purchased. If there are commercial photographers or photographic stylists in your area, let them know what items you can provide.

A floral designer or artist might offer to decorate a local restaurant. Civic buildings frequently have temporary exhibits of local products or artwork on display. The owner of a nursery could rent out a specially designed area for garden weddings, and can arrange for ancillary services, such as catering and music.

Tip 79

Place your ads in newspapers and magazines, or distribute flyers

The particular type of business you have will determine what kind of advertising will effectively reach your potential clients or customers. For some businesses, no mass-market advertising is necessary; personal contact and word-of-mouth, or advertising in a trade paper, might be sufficient. But even if you provide a specialized service, you do need to find the audience that you need to target.

You can invest as little or as much in advertising as you think will be effective. The Small Business Administration suggests 3 to 5 percent of your annual revenue, although this could be adjusted up or down

To help you focus on how advertising can work best for you, here's the Small Business Administration's Advertising Blueprint:

1. What are your overall goals?

2. Which marketing tools will help you achieve them?

3. What is the purpose of your advertising program? (Be specific.)

4. What is your advertising budget?

5. What are the most important features and benefits of your product/service?

6. Who is your target audience? (Create a profile of your best customer.)

7. Who is your competition?

8. How are you perceived relative to your competition?

9. What identity or personality do you want to project?

10. What is the single most important benefit you want to convey about your product/service?

11. What other benefits set you apart from the competition?

12. What advertising tools will you use?

Yellow Pages	Newspapers	Magazines
Radio/TV	Direct Mail	Telemarketing
Billboards	Signage	Other

13. How will you measure the effectiveness of your advertising program?

depending on the advertising done by your competition and the limitations of your budget.

Flyers are probably the least-expensive way to spread your message. Just remember that it's against federal law to put them in mailboxes. As an alternative, for example, landscaping services might leave plastic bags—weighted with gravel and containing a flyer, price list, or business card—on doorsteps. And we've all received hang-tags that fit over doorknobs. Flyers put on the windshields of cars parked at certain locations and events can also be very effective, especially if your demographic analysis indicates there's a market for you among people who frequent that particular location. For example, if your product would appeal to college students, your flyers could be distributed in university parking lots.

Paid advertising in local newspapers (either classified or display ads) is often quite reasonable. And don't forget the Yellow Pages, or a bold-faced listing in the white pages.

You can control where, when, and how often your message will appear, how it will look, and what it will say. You can target your audience by the media you choose. You'll pay less per ad in newspapers and magazines by contracting to run several insertions over a period of time, rather than deciding whether to advertise as each issue goes to press. If you prepare several ads at once, you can save on production costs and view all the ads together to make sure they are consistent. A recurring theme or tag line and the cumulative effect of seeing or hearing your ads more than once will help people remember what you have to offer.

Newspapers and magazines may have theme issues, advertising supplements, or promotional coverage such as special sections featuring real estate, investing, or home and garden improvement. Schools often run advertising for local businesses in their event programs and special publications. These ads target a particular audience, which may be the group you want to reach.

If you sell merchandise produced by someone else, you can stretch your advertising budget by taking advantage of co-op programs. Generally, the manufacturer will pay for a portion of the costs of mailer production and media space and time. Their contribution is usually based on the quantity of merchandise you purchase from them for resale. Every medium, from the Yellow Pages to print ads, radio to TV, qualifies for co-op advertising. The Yellow Pages Publishers Association publishes *The Co-op Handbook*, a twice-yearly directory of thousands of co-op program listings. Indexed by brand name and company, each listing provides the company name, the type of plan it offers, whether mention of competitors in an ad is allowed, and the type and size of ads required.

Other media to consider are billboards, bus and bus-stop signage, shopping bags, and point-of-sale displays. Telemarketing is a way to locate prospective sales leads.

Tip 80

Decide if your ads would be effective on local radio or television

Community television and radio stations offer reasonably priced ways to advertise; this is a good option if you know that your target audience overlaps with their viewers and listeners. Again, you'll pay less per ad by contracting to run several spots over a period of time. Work with the representatives of the station to put together effective ads, or hire a professional.

Some communities have "bulletin board" TV channels that post public-service messages and also run advertising messages for local businesses.

Tip 81

Design advertising that's effective

Unless you are an advertising expert yourself, hire a professional designer and/or copywriter, or work closely with the advertising rep for the media you choose. You'll save time and effort, and you will maximize the value of the ad space or time you're purchasing.

Good ads rely on the "Three-I" principle: Involve, Inform, and Illustrate.

- *Involve:* Arouse curiosity, lure them in, and invite them to participate. It's commonly called "pushing their buttons."

- *Inform:* Answer the question, "What's in it for me?" How will your product or service make the user happier, healthier, or wealthier? Even intangibles or "secret motivators" such as status, self-enhancement, or peace of mind should be considered. If you're a financial consultant, explain how your service will improve the client's bottom line.

- *Illustrate:* Show both the product and its benefits in an appropriate setting. For example, if you're a personal trainer, show an attractive, athletic person (maybe yourself) to illustrate the benefits of your service.

Measure your results to evaluate the success of your advertising campaign. Although most advertising aims at sustained returns over time, there are ways to get instant feedback. If your print ad includes a coupon with an expiration date, or an announcement of a limited offer, you should get a measurable response right away. For best results, the price break should be at least 15 percent. However, one theory holds that coupons draw people who only buy at a discount and never become repeat customers, so it's important to monitor the results. Be sure to ask new customers how they heard about you to see what's working.

Tip 82

Participate in trade shows

Trade shows are excellent vehicles for introducing new products and meeting potential buyers. If you belong to a trade association or other networking group, you will be able to keep yourself informed of the trade shows that involve your type of product or service. Especially if you are not selling your product at the retail level, trade shows are one of the best ways to introduce it to department-store buyers, distributors/wholesalers, mail-order catalog merchandisers, and other quantity purchasers.

Booth space is generally not too expensive: $13 per square foot, on average, with the typical small booth covering 100 square feet. Even small companies can usually afford attractive displays. With creative marketing and good booth design, a small business can actually appear as substantial as the larger corporations. However, don't expect to make enough sales at a show to cover its cost. The idea is to generate future sales.

Expect to pay $2,000 to $5,000 (exclusive of tabletop displays) to have a booth made to fit a 10 × 10-foot space (the usual minimum you can rent). The display should be collapsible so that you can take it on a plane. Renting a similar booth costs about one-third as much, so if you use it three times a year, buying is probably worth the investment. Your design should be clean and uncluttered, and able to attract passersby in five to fifteen seconds. It needn't be high-tech with a lot of bells and whistles; just be sure that what you are offering is clear and that the image you hope to project comes through.

Consider regional shows, which can bring you into contact with qualified prospects you might not otherwise meet; they usually cost less than national shows, provide market-research opportunities, and may place you where you have few competitors. On the local level, there are often opportunities to exhibit at trade fairs right in your own community. You

The Small Business Administration offers these "Guidelines for Good Boothmanship."

1. Tell your sales team [your booth people, who may be friends, relatives, or part-time help you hire just for the show] why you decided to attend this particular show and what you hope to gain from it. The better they understand your motives, the better they will convey the right message to prospective customers.

2. Never have your booth people sit. If they need to rest, let them leave the booth. In fact, if you don't even have chairs in your booth, no one will be tempted to use them.

3. Never eat in the booth. Out of politeness, most potential customers will walk by, rather than interrupt someone's meal. Besides, it looks terrible. Also, don't drink or smoke in the booth.

4. Don't bring a phone into the booth. When you're on the phone, you discourage people from entering your exhibit area.

could even organize this type of event if there isn't one already. Home-improvement expos, hobby shows, garden shows, and arts-and-crafts festivals are all opportunities to present yourself and your product.

It pays to do some preshow publicity by phone or mail to let your current customers and new prospects know that you will be an exhibitor. At a good-sized show, attendees know that they have to make the most of their time and can't always visit every booth, so they plan

5. Be sure your booth people know your products or services well. If there is a product to demonstrate, let them practice prior to the show.

6. Give your helpers specific goals, such as garnering a certain number of sales leads. This gives them something tangible to strive for during the event.

7. Salespeople tend to like to bond with customers. While that's fine with traditional selling, it's deadly at a trade show. Train your people so they feel comfortable giving a quick presentation and then moving on to the next person.

8. Don't let your booth staff improvise. Have them memorize a sales spiel so they can efficiently and effectively convey your message.

9. Set up a system for qualifying leads, and train your people in using it.

10. Be judicious when handing out literature. Most of it ends up in the trash can unread.

ahead. You want to make sure that you are on their list of booths to visit, so send an announcement in advance that describes any new products you will be introducing and lets them know that you look forward to seeing them at your booth.

At business-to-business shows, selling on the show floor is usually not allowed, so exhibitors participate for the purpose of generating sales leads. You have to find out quickly if the people visiting your booth are qualified leads. There's not much point in launching into your sales presentation if the prospect is not a likely buyer. Ask if he already sells products similar to yours. If so, which brands? Would he be interested in hearing more about your product? If he answers that the product is too expensive or that he's completely satisfied with his current lines, you don't want to spend as much time with this prospect as with someone else who seems more receptive. At consumer shows, which do allow selling, exhibitors expect to generate sales and introduce new products directly to end users.

It's extremely important to follow up on the new contacts you make at a show, and the sooner the better. Answer any questions they may have raised, and thank them for visiting your display.

Before you take the leap and rent booth space at a show, attend as many shows as you can to see what works and doesn't work for exhibitors.

Tip 83

Review your business plan and make adjustments

A review will help you to focus on your goals and objectives and keep you on track. It's usually best to concentrate on a "core" service or product, rather than diffusing your effectiveness by attempting to branch out into too many other areas. Put your primary effort into the mainstay of your home business.

However, from time to time, you may want to make adjustments—we all need to be flexible. MIT economist David Birch coined the term "gazelle" to describe a business that moves at a lightning pace and has the agility to switch directions the instant it spots a new opportunity. Gazelles have three basic qualities:

- They rapidly spot marketing opportunities and explore them.
- They constantly improve productivity and efficiency.
- They can quickly change and expand organizational structures as appropriate.

Successful businesses establish goals and regularly take stock to see if those goals are being met. You need to determine the best marketing maneuvers, tax strategies, plans for expansion, and personal objectives. Then you need to review them on an ongoing basis to make adjustments that will help you accomplish what you have set out to do.

Tip **84**

Plan ahead—use calendars and a tickler file

Set up a filing system with separate folders for each month of the year, so you can file incoming information as you receive it for future review at the beginning of each appropriate month. You might want to have files for more than just the current year, so material can be moved forward from one year to the next. When you review the contents of your file at the beginning of each month, you can decide whether you should look at the information now or move it forward to another month—or next year.

If your business is seasonal, mark your calendar with reminders of when to order materials, when to place your advertising, and other important information. If you can take early-bird discounts and save on shipping by ordering in advance, this will help you to maximize your profits. If you wait until the last minute, expedited freight charges will take a bite out of your profit, or you might not be able to find sources for the things you need.

As each month is completed, file its calendar page in next year's file folder so you can refer back to it. We recently took on a number of projects that all became due in October, so we had to remind ourselves that if we make the same commitments again, we'll need to stagger the deadlines or be careful not to take on more than we can reasonably handle.

Tip 85

Set up a system for paying bills on time

An Internal Revenue Service tax calendar is available via the Internet (see page 127). It will help you plan ahead for monthly, quarterly, and annual tax payments. This calendar (or a similar one) can also be used to help you remember payments that are routinely due quarterly, semi-annually, and annually, such as insurance or other important or major expenses. Especially if you operate on a tight-cash-flow basis, this will serve to remind you well in advance of large expenses coming due.

An accordion file divided into monthly sections is handy for filing incoming bills, and keeps them in one place for reference when you are ready to make payments. When bills arrive, put the payment stub that you will send with your check into the return envelope, note the due date on your bill-paying calendar, and file it in the appropriate month's "accounts payable" file. The statement itself, with details of your expenditures for your tax return, can be filed immediately in the proper folder for future reference. Once a week, or another appropriate interval, write checks for any payments coming due. For some people, a good system is to write checks in advance for the whole month, stamp the envelopes and indicate the mailing date somewhere on the envelope or inside the flap, and then mail them at the appropriate time.

Whatever system you use, allow plenty of time for payments to reach creditors, so you won't pay interest or late-payment penalties needlessly (seven to ten business days is the interval recommended by one large credit-card company). However, if you are penalized for a late payment, call the company and explain that the delay was inadvertent; chances are the late charge will be waived if you have an otherwise good record for prompt payment.

Tip 86

Do administrative chores efficiently

Develop a schedule and try to do routine tasks at a particular time each day, week, or month. Link those boring but necessary administrative chores to something you enjoy—listen to music while you're filing, or have a leisurely cup of herbal tea while you open and sort your mail. We know a doctor who reads professional journals while she works out on her exercise bike. Always take along busywork that you can do when you're waiting for a client or when you have some free time between appointments.

When you open mail, discard the envelope and any advertising inserts you don't need, and just keep what's important. Don't let things get misplaced, or you'll waste time looking for them. But prioritize; don't waste time filing material you won't need. Some efficiency experts suggest segregating material into three piles: pertinent stuff to keep and file as soon as possible; items to set aside until you can read them, and then decide whether to keep them or not; and things you might need but that are questionable—put these in a "maybe" file and periodically sort through it. Chances are, if you haven't dug out items from this last batch since you first got them, you don't need them and they can be tossed into the recycling bin. In this age of ever-changing information and technology, the majority of the material with which we are bombarded becomes obsolete, or at least stale, very quickly. If you have a tendency to accumulate too much material, you'll just have to deal with it later.

Any filing system is only as good as it is useable. First, file or store only what you need to keep, in such a way that you can retrieve it when it's needed. If space is at a premium, pack obsolete files, label them, and banish them to dead storage, off-site in a rented storage unit—if it is necessary to keep them at all. We know an attorney who uses a fax machine to send documents to his computer, where they are electronically filed for future reference. He keeps very few hard copies in his conventional filing system. A scanner would serve the same purpose.

In any case, try to handle paperwork as few times as possible, and do as much of a particular kind of routine task at one sitting as you can.

Tip 87

Fight the tendency to procrastinate

Make daily, weekly, and monthly "To Do" lists. For many of us, just writing down things helps to set priorities and emphasize what's important, even if we don't work down the list item-by-item. Others like to make checklists and get great satisfaction by crossing off each task accomplished. But be careful not to let the list-making itself become another chore. The planners that have become so popular in the past few years sometimes come with a training course for their use, which makes them a valuable organizational tool for many users.

Try not to let yourself get sidetracked and distracted. It might help to set time-frame goals: Accomplish such-and-such before lunch; do this-or-that chore and then walk the dog or stroll to the park. Race against the clock just to see how much you can get done in a given amount of time. Set artificial deadlines if you don't have real ones— think of how nice it would be to finish a project early and then have time to do other things you enjoy.

Attack your least favorite chores first to get them out of the way. Or, if you're really having a hard time getting to something you dislike doing, start with something more appealing just to get your creative juices flowing.

Working at home requires a tremendous amount of self-discipline, especially for those of us who set our own schedules, because there are always a lot of distractions. Each of us has to develop a method for maximizing a workday, especially if we don't have client appointments or other time constraints that serve to structure our time.

Tip 88

Set up a workable system for keeping track of contacts

Collect business cards and put them in clear plastic three-ring binder sheets made for this purpose. These pages can be arranged with dividers labeled by subject matter, geography, or whatever works for you. This system works well for contacts that you don't expect to refer to regularly, but still want to keep.

Alternatively, use a rotary card-file system (such as Roladex) for frequent contacts. Keep blank cards handy near your telephone and computer to jot down street and e-mail addresses and telephone numbers. File the cards by company name, or by subject if you aren't likely to remember the person's or company's name. Use a system with file cards that are large enough to staple business cards to them. This also leaves room for you to write additional notes, such as when you last spoke to them.

Tip 89

Color-code your filing system

Lisa M. Roberts, author of *How to Raise a Family and a Career Under One Roof*, suggests using different colors for different types of files, depending on their status or function. Her choices are:

- *Green:* Finances: bookkeeping, collections

- *Blue:* Administration: correspondence, filing, phone, and mail lists

- *Yellow:* Production: current projects

- *Red:* Sales: promotion, marketing

If you have only a few projects going at one time, use a different color for each one. One idea is to keep current files in colored, clear plastic legal-size envelopes with string closures, using a different color for each client or project. You can see what's inside, and everything stays together in the proper envelope. If you've put sticky notes on your paperwork, they're not likely to be peeled off accidentally and lost.

Tip 90

Establish a line of credit and a "business only" credit-card account

Open an account with your bank or credit union that allows you to get cash advances from time to time when you need them. Don't borrow unless and until you need to, and repay the loan promptly. If you take out a conventional loan, you will pay interest on the entire amount from the date of the loan. However, if you don't need a lump sum, a line of credit will enable you to pay interest only on the amount you currently owe.

Don't comingle your personal purchases and your business expenses. Earmark one credit card for the business and keep those charges separate. Interest you pay on business credit-card purchases is tax-deductible, so you will need records to back up that expense.

Tip 91

Hit up Uncle Sam for a loan

The federal government's Small Business Innovative Research (SBIR) program, run by the Small Business Administration on behalf of ten federal agencies, lends $1 billion each year to businesses seeking to develop products that might be useful to the government. The Defense Department is interested in products for the armed forces, but the money also comes from the Departments of Agriculture, Commerce, Education, Energy, Transportation, and Health and Human Services, as well as NASA, the Environmental Protection Agency, and the National Science Foundation. The only string attached to the loan is that the SBIR has a license to use your product royalty-free for five years, during which you are free to sell your product to other customers and receive all profits. The paperwork and separate accounting procedures required might seem daunting, but the rewards can be worthwhile. Contact the SBA or visit the Web site: www.sba.gov/SBIR.

Tip 92

Develop strategies for financial fitness

You need an accurate estimate of your volume of business and how it might fluctuate over a year's time. This way, you can adjust for seasonal variations and project your high- and low-income periods. Part of this equation is how your type of product or service is usually paid for: Do clients pay on receipt or completion of the project, or is a thirty-, sixty-, or ninety-day cycle customary? You also have to consider pricing: If it takes a certain number of days to complete a job, your price has to be worth the time it takes to get it done. However, if you are a contractor, there are times when it might make sense to cut prices, such as during slack periods or just to keep a crew employed so they won't seek work elsewhere. Experience will teach you just how much leeway you can afford.

Expenses are another item in your cash-flow calculations. The costs of providing a product or service and the overhead costs of operating a business are obvious expenses for all businesses. In the case of the home-based business, the portion of household expenses allocated to a home office, studio, or workshop must be considered part of the business overhead.

Tip 93

Get what's coming to you

With the stress put on personal relationships for the small-business owner, having a good collection system in place can help you reduce your outstanding accounts without alienating your customers. This is particularly true if you frequently work on speculation or contingency, and if you carry open accounts for your clients and customers.

Business transactions should be documented with written estimates, confirmation letters, records of meetings and phone calls, and detailed invoices complete with payment terms. Statements should be provided on a monthly or other appropriate basis, to prevent accounts in arrears from falling through the cracks. Expensive, custom, and long-term projects should be covered by contracts that specify initial deposits, interim or progress payments, and final payments.

Reminder letters should be sent as soon as a payment is missed; the longer you wait, the less your chances of receiving what's due you. Don't be argumentative or threatening at first. Make sure the customer is satisfied; if there is a reason he is withholding payment, attempt to resolve the problem. If he is having financial difficulties, offer to set up a payment schedule that he can live with, and get a commitment. Your second letter should be firmer than the first, and the third, if necessary, should let him know that you will seek legal action unless he responds within ten days. Then, follow through! Remember, you can only threaten once.

Your legal remedies are small-claims court, hiring an attorney, or hiring a collection agency. To file in small-claims court, the dollar amount of your dispute must fall within certain guidelines, which vary by state. But winning your case is not the same as getting paid. The court does not enforce its judgments and collect your money for you.

If you have retained an attorney for other purposes (which is a good idea anyway), you might be able to combine his collection services with other fees. A collection agency will use intimidating letters and phone calls to try to get debts paid, and will charge 25 to 50 percent of the amount collected. Some will charge only if they are successful in collecting the debt.

Preferably, you will avoid the possibility of uncollectible receivables by reducing the risk in the first place. Don't offer credit, and do offer incentives such as discounts for cash payment. Request credit references, and check them out. Offer to accept payment by credit card; you will pay a fee to the credit-card company, but the company assumes the responsibility for collection. Or, ask your customers for credit-card information and have a written and signed understanding that any accounts sixty days in arrears will be charged to their credit card.

Tip 94

Open a merchant account to accept credit-card payments

Accepting credit-card payment will help you avoid having to make your own debt collections. Customers will likely be attracted to the convenience of paying with "plastic." Check around for the best rate so that you aren't paying too much for this service. Your source might be your own bank, a savings and loan, a thrift, or a credit union. Financial institutions have very stringent requirements for granting merchant accounts, so find out what information will be required with your application. Trade associations or local business organizations sometimes provide Visa and Mastercard accounts as a member service.

Merchant service providers or independent selling organizations (ISOs) act as intermediaries in setting up merchant accounts between small businesses and banks. Although some might not charge all of the following, expect to pay application fees up to about $200; per-transaction charges up to 25 cents; monthly statement fees up to about $10; and voice-authorization fees (when you phone to verify a cardholder's credit) up to about $1. You should investigate the company and verify its standing with the bank it deals through.

Another option for obtaining a merchant account is to apply directly to a credit-card company such as American Express or Novus/Discovery.

Tip 95

Manage your inventory

Don't overstock at the wrong time of year. You don't want to pay for and store material that won't be used for months. However, you also don't want to pay top dollar for supplies, so learn the best time to buy certain items.

Al Gorin, a contractor, comments that he always used to have odds and ends of construction materials left over at the end of a job, which he stored in boxes in his garage. Unfortunately, he didn't have an inventory-recording system, so when he needed the items for a later project, he never knew where anything was and had to go out and purchase more. He finally decided that it was better to sell most of his leftovers than try to store them for future use.

Tip 96

Try to avoid "feast or famine" cycles

If your business is highly seasonal, try to offset that seasonality by coming up with a midyear sales strategy. If "Christmas in July" works for you, go for it!

Tom Arnessen, a certified public accountant, had the usual tax-preparer's work schedule: a heavy load for four months, ending with the mid-April tax-filing deadline. It didn't seem to make sense to hire help for the busy season in order to increase his clientele, only to have several slow months afterward. Tom's solution was to file extensions for his clients and spread out the tax-preparation season until August 15. Now he can give personal service to all of his clients, and he has expanded his high season from four to eight months.

Tip 97

Keep your books balanced

Good records will provide the information you need to keep an eye on how your business is functioning, as well as assist you in making better short- and long-term decisions.

Your bookkeeping system should be simple enough to manage with a minimum of time and effort. You need records of sales and operating results, fixed and variable costs, profit and loss, inventory and supply information, and credit and collection totals. You will need information for periodic tax returns and reports to regulatory agencies. As part of your long-term planning, you'll need comparisons with previous years' operations, forecasts, and budgets.

You can elect to use either the cash or accrual method of accounting. With the cash method, income is reported the same year it is received and expenses deducted the same year they are paid. With an accrual system, income is reported the year it is earned, even if payment hasn't been received. Cash-basis accounting is the system usually used by sole proprietorships and partnerships, due to its simplicity. However, if inventory is involved, the IRS requires that you use the accrual method. Whichever accounting method you choose, it will probably also be used for tax purposes.

Unless you are in the accounting or tax business yourself, work with a professional to set up your system.

Tip 98

Find an accounting system you will actually use

Whether you choose to keep your own set of ledgers, a simple accounting entry system available at any office-supply store, or accounting software, choose a system that you understand and will use. If number crunching isn't your forte, hire a part-time bookkeeper to come in periodically and take care of it for you, or consult an accountant who can set up your system and monitor it for you. Ask for recommendations from

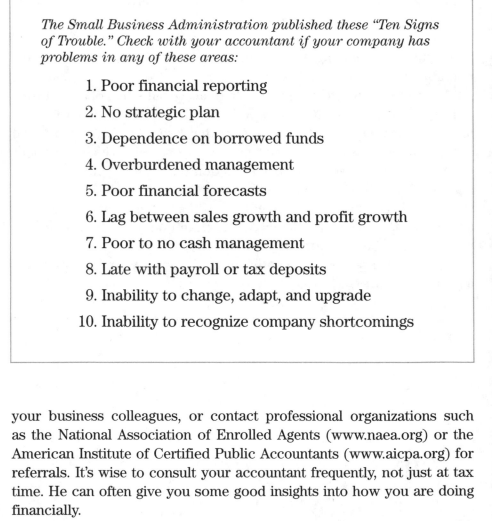

The Small Business Administration published these "Ten Signs of Trouble." Check with your accountant if your company has problems in any of these areas:

1. Poor financial reporting

2. No strategic plan

3. Dependence on borrowed funds

4. Overburdened management

5. Poor financial forecasts

6. Lag between sales growth and profit growth

7. Poor to no cash management

8. Late with payroll or tax deposits

9. Inability to change, adapt, and upgrade

10. Inability to recognize company shortcomings

your business colleagues, or contact professional organizations such as the National Association of Enrolled Agents (www.naea.org) or the American Institute of Certified Public Accountants (www.aicpa.org) for referrals. It's wise to consult your accountant frequently, not just at tax time. He can often give you some good insights into how you are doing financially.

Another reason for keeping your records in order is that the IRS expects you to be able to prove that you're running a business, not just indulging in a hobby. Records and receipts will justify your expenses, even if you're not showing a profit yet. For example, authors should collect rejection letters to prove that they have submitted their work to publishers; contractors need to keep estimates they've submitted, even if they didn't get the jobs.

Tip 99

Use a software management program

The main advantage of a computerized accounting program is the ability to instantly generate reports, pie charts, and other useful summaries of where you stand this year, comparisons with past years, and so on.

You might shop for a simple checkbook system appropriate for an uncomplicated business. Retailers might prefer a system with cash-drawer, bar-code, and inventory functions built in. Manufacturers' software includes inventory, value-added, and cost-per-unit accounting. Consulting and service companies might need a system with job-costing, estimating, and tracking functions to allocate billable hours and expenses by client or product.

A small-business accounting package can cost less than $200. Choose a system that will stay ahead of your company's increasing size and complexity, and upgrade sooner rather than later. Your accountant can help you by suggesting the kinds of information that the software package should be able to handle. You can choose to run the whole program yourself, or just enter the data and rely on your accountant to check it and generate financial reports.

Tip 100

Take a write-off on excess inventory

Don't hang on to unprofitable merchandise or supplies. You might be taking space and effort from activities that would produce better results.

Sell your excess stuff on eBay (the Internet auction site), or donate it to charity. Take books and magazines to used-book stores, local hospitals, or convalescent homes. Clear out prototypes that didn't work, "dogs" that didn't sell, and obsolete equipment, manuals, and materials. Schools have particularly tight budgets for computer equipment and art supplies, so donate what you can. Keep track of any donations and take a tax write-off.

Tip 101

Keep your business small and manageable

Once you've successfully found and exploited your niche, you will no doubt have a loyal group of customers who are happy doing business with your company. Will they stick with you if your business becomes larger, and perhaps less personalized? If you become a bigger operation, you will be competing with large stores or chain businesses on *their* playing field, and you might not be ready for that kind of competition.

Growing larger probably means that you will need to hire additional help, and perhaps you don't really want to become a manager with employees to oversee, hire, and fire. The federal and state governments have set up regulations for protecting employees, and this entails more paperwork and taxes for employers.

Should you opt to condense your activities, you may have to make some hard choices in order to limit your scope. If you have expanded into a number of different areas, perhaps it would be wise to analyze each and divest yourself of some of them. Are you spreading yourself too thin? By limiting the number of different facets of your business, you can maximize the effectiveness of those that seem to do best, or focus your attention on the ones you prefer to stay involved in.

Delegate or sell off some of your activities. It's a good idea anyway to have colleagues you trust and to whom you can refer business when you are overburdened. If you can farm out some of your operation, you can still keep in touch with those functions in your area of expertise. Someone in another geographic location might be interested in operating a branch of your business.

Recommended Reading

Anderson, Sandy. *The Work at Home Balancing Act: The Professional Resource Guide for Managing Yourself, Your Work, and Your Family at Home.* New York; Avon Books, 1998.

Attard, Janet. *Business Know-How: An Operational Guide for Home-Based and Micro-Sized Businesses With Limited Budgets.* Holbrook, Mass.: Adams Media, 1999.

———. *The Home Office and Small Business Answer Book: Solutions to the Most Frequently Asked Questions About Starting and Running Your Business.* New York: Henry Holt, 2000.

Axman, Andi, and David H. Bangs Jr. *Work at Home Wisdom: A Collection of Quips, Tips and Inspirations to Balance Work, Family and Home.* Dover, N.H.: Upstart Publishing, 1998.

Baker, Sunny, and Kim Baker. *The Ultimate Home Office Survival Guide.* New York: Peterson's Guides, 1998.

Bewsey, Susan. *Start and Run a Profitable House Cleaning Business.* Bellingham, Wash.: Self-Counsel Press, 1999.

———. *The Crafts Business Answer Book & Resource Guide: Answers to Hundreds of Troublesome Questions About Starting, Marketing, and Managing a Homebased Business.* Cincinnati, Ohio: M. Evans & Co., 1998.

Brabec, Barbara. *Make It Profitable: How to Make Your Art, Craft, Design, Writing, or Publishing Business More Efficient, More Satisfying, and More Profitable.* Cincinnati, Ohio: M. Evans & Co., 2000.

Bredin, Alice, and Kirsten M. Lagatree. *The Home Office Solution: How to Balance Your Professional and Personal Lives While Working at Home.* New York: John Wiley & Sons, 1998.

Carter, Gary W. *J.K. Lasser's Taxes Made Easy for Home-Based Business.* Foster City, Calif.: McMillan General Reference, 2000.

Chan, James. *Spare Room Tycoon: Succeeding Independently, The 70 Lessons of Sane Self-Employment.* Sonoma, Calif.: Nicholas Brealey, 2000.

Cook, Mel. *Home Business, Big Business: The Definitive Guide to Starting and Operating On-Line and Traditional Home-Based Ventures.* Foster City, Calif.: IDG Books Worldwide, 1998.

Cunningham, J. Barton, Ph.D. *The Stress Management Sourcebook.* Los Angeles: Lowell House, 1997.

Davidson, Jeffrey P. *Marketing for the Home-Based Business*. Holbrook, Mass.: Adams Media, 1999.

Devi, Nischala Joy. *The Healing Path of Yoga: Time-Honored Wisdom and Scientifically Proven Methods That Alleviate Stress, Open Your Heart, and Enrich Your Life*. New York: Three Rivers Press, 2000.

Edwards, Paul, et al. *Getting Business to Come to You: A Complete Do-It-Yourself Guide to Attracting All the Business You Can Enjoy*, 2d ed. New York: Putnam Publishing Group, 1998.

Edwards, Paul, Sarah Edwards, and Peter Economy. *Home-Based Business for Dummies*. Indianapolis, Ind.: IDG Books Worldwide, 2000.

Edwards, Paul and Sarah. *Outfitting Your Home Business for Much Less*. New York: AMA COM, 2000.

———. *Working from Home: Everything You Need to Know About Living and Working Under the Same Roof*, 5th ed. New York: J. P. Tarcher, 1999.

Eisenberg, Ronnie. *Organize Your Home Office: Simple Routines for Setting Up an Office at Home*. New York: Hyperion, 2000.

Garner, Alan. *Conversationally Speaking: Tested New Ways to Increase Your Personal and Social Effectiveness*. Los Angeles: Lowell House, 1997.

Gordon, Kim T. *Bringing Home the Business: The 30 Truths Every Home Business Owner Must Know*. New York: Perigee, 2000.

Gould, Meredith. *Tips for Your Home Office (Enhancing Your Life at Home)*. Williamstown, Mass.: Storey Books, 1998.

———. *Working from Home: 500 Tips and Strategies for Success*. Williamstown, Mass.: Storey Books, 2000.

Gregory, Shirley Siluk. *The Home Team: How to Live, Love & Work at Home*. Navarre, Fla.: Bookhome Publishing, 1999.

Harlan, Michael, and Linda Harlan. *Growing Profits: How to Start and Operate a Backyard Nursery*. White River Junction, Vt.: Chelsea Green, 1998.

Heady, Christy, and Janet Bernstel. *The Complete Idiot's Guide to Making Money in Freelancing*. White River Junction, Vt.: Complete Idiot's Guides, McMillan Distribution, 1998.

Hemphill, Barbara. *Taming the Paper Tiger at Work*, Washington, D.C.: Kiplinger Books, 1998.

Henry, Maxye, and Lou Henry. *The Home-Business Sourcebook: Everything You Need to Know About Starting and Running a Business from Home*. Los Angeles: Lowell House, 1998.

Hull, Caroline, and Tanya Wallace. *Moneymaking Moms: How Work at Home Can Work for You*. Secaucus, N.J.: Citadel Press, 1998.

Kanarek, Lisa A. *Organizing Your Home Office for Success: Expert Strategies That Can Work for You.* Dallas, Tex.: Blakely Press, 1998.

Kern, Coralee Smith, and Tammara Hoffman Wolfgram. *Run Your Own Home Business (Here's How).* Lincolnwood, Ill.: NTC Publishing Group, 1998.

Kishel, Gregory F., and Patricia Gunter Kishel. *Start, Run, and Profit from Your Own Home-Based Business*, 2d ed. New York: John Wiley & Sons, 1999.

Lagatree, Kirsten M. *Feng Shui at Work: Arranging Your Work Space for Peak Performance and Maximum Profit.* New York: Villard Books, 1998.

LeBoeuf, Michael. *The Perfect Business: How to Make a Million from Home With No Payroll, No Employee Headaches, No Debts and No Sleepless Nights!* New York: Fireside, 1996.

Levinson, Jay Conrad, and Kathryn Tyler. *Guerrilla Saving: Secrets for Keeping Profits in Your Home-Based Business.* New York: John Wiley & Sons, 2000.

Lonier, Terry. *Working Solo: The Real Guide to Freedom & Financial Success with Your Own Business*, 2d ed. New York: John Wiley & Sons, 1998.

Lumpkin, Emily S. *Get Paid to Shop: Be a Personal Shopper for Corporate America.* Columbia, S.C.: Forte Publishing, 1999.

Matthias, Rebecca. *MothersWork.* Garden City, N.Y.: Doubleday, 1999.

Monaghan, Kelly. *Home-Based Travel Agent: How to Cash in on the Exciting New World of Travel Marketing.* New York: Intrepid Traveler, 1999.

Murphy, Donna M. *Organize Your Books in 6 Easy Steps: A Workbook for the Sole Proprietor Service-Oriented Business.* Fort Collins, Colo.: IRIE Publishing, 1998.

Paul, Donna. *The Home Office Book.* New York: Artisan, 1996.

Pruissen, Catherine M. *Start and Run a Profitable Home Day Care.* Bellingham, Wash.: Self-Counsel Press, 1999.

Ray, Norm. *Smart Tax Write-Offs: Hundreds of Tax Deduction Ideas for Home-Based Businesses, Independent Contractors, All Entrepreneurs.* Windsor, Calif.: Rayve Productions, 1999.

Roberts, Lisa. *How to Raise a Family and a Career Under One Roof: A Parent's Guide to Home Business.* Moon Township, Pa.: Bookhaven Press, 1997.

Shaw, Lisa. *How to Publish from Your Home: Everything You Need to Know to Successfully Publish Books, Newsletters, Web Sites, Greeting Cards and Software.* Rockland, Calif.: Prima Publishing, 2000.

Shimberg, Elaine Fantle. *Write Where You Live: Successful Freelancing at Home Without Driving Yourself and Your Family Crazy.* Cincinnati, Ohio: Writers Digest Books, 1999.

Shulem, Julie. *Home-Based Business Mom: A Basic Guide to Time Management and Organization for the Working Woman.* Santa Barbara, Calif.: Newhoff Publishing, 1998.

Simmons, Terry. *How to Own and Operate Your Own Home Day Care Business Successfully Without Going Nuts! The Day Care Survival Handbook and Guide for Aspiring Home Day Care.* Phoenix, Ariz.: Amber Books, 1999.

Stankus, Jan. *How to Own and Operate a Bed & Breakfast* (Home-Based Business Series). Old Saybrook, Conn.: Globe Pequot Press, 2000.

Sumner, Holly, Ph.D. *Meditation Sourcebook: Meditation for Mortals.* Los Angeles: Lowell House, 2000.

Taylor, T. M. *Secrets to a Successful Greenhouse and Business: A complete Guide to Starting and Operating a High-Profit Organic or Hydroponic Business That's Beneficial to the Environment.* Melbourne, Fla.: Greenearth Publishing Co., 2000.

Zbar, Jeffery D. *Home Office Know-How.* Chicago, Ill.: Upstart Publishing Co., 1998.

Zelinsky, Marilyn. *Practical Home Office Solutions.* New York: McGraw-Hill, 1998.

Small Business
Tax Help from the IRS

The IRS is now under Congressional mandate to be more responsive to taxpayers' needs. While some taxpayers may not have noticed a change, the IRS has become kinder and friendlier, at least on a modest scale, in the last few years. Here are some of the services, publications, and assistance available.

Assistance

Small Business Administration Business Information Centers (BICs). The IRS and SBA have entered into an agreement to support the small-business community by distributing key IRS business tax forms and publications in all fifty-seven BIC sites and seventeen One Stop Capital Shops. In addition, the IRS is piloting a program where IRS tax specialists will provide one-on-one assistance at selected BIC locations in Los Angeles, Chicago, Boston, and Atlanta. For more information, contact your local IRS office in these cities and ask for the taxpayer education coordinator.

Small-business tax workshops. Through a partnership between the IRS and local organizations, workshops are available on topics including starting a business, recordkeeping, preparing business tax returns, self-employment tax issues, employment taxes, and other aspects of running your business. Call your local IRS taxpayer education coordinator about the workshops.

Publications

The IRS has a number of useful publications that are suitable for small-business owners.

They include:

- Publication 1: *Your Rights as a Taxpayer.* Informs taxpayers of their rights and includes information on the examination and collection process.

- Publication 334: *Tax Guide for Small Businesses.* Basic federal tax info for small-business owners.

- Publication 454: *Your Business Tax Kit.* Contains various business tax forms and publications.

- Publication 583: *Starting a Business and Keeping Records.* Provides basic federal tax information for people who are starting a business. Gives good information on record keeping.

- Publication 910: *Guide to Free Tax Services.* Explains many free tax services, publications, and forms the IRS has available for individuals, businesses, and organizations; and tells how these services and products can be obtained.

- Publication 954: *Tax Incentives for Empowerment Zones and Other Distressed Communities.* Explains the tax incentives available to businesses that establish themselves or operate in these areas.

- Publication 1518: *Tax Calendar for Small Businesses.* This twelve-month wall calendar shows due dates for making payroll deposits, paying estimated taxes, and filing major business-tax forms. It includes information on business tax law and IRS notices and penalties, and provides bookkeeping and record-keeping tips. Visit the IRS Web site at www.irs.ustreas.gov/prod/tax_edu/tax_cal.

- Publication 3207: *Small Business Resource Guide: What You Need to Know About Taxes and Other Topics.* This CD-ROM is designed to provide small business entrepreneurs with most of the information and products they might need to meet their regulatory requirements. The CD-ROM has been distributed to all the SBA's BIC sites. Call 1-800-U-ASK-SBA for the nearest location.

Services

The IRS provides twenty-four-hour accessibility to electronic information. You can download and print more than 600 federal tax forms with instructions and ninety publications. Many tax research tools are available, including tax regulations, more than 150 tax topics, frequently asked questions, statistical studies, important changes, newsletters, and much more. Most of the information is available on the Internet at www.irs.ustreas.gov. You can order forms and publications at no charge by calling 1-800-829-3676.

From a fax machine, you can dial IRS Tax Fax at (703) 368-9694 and follow the voice prompts to get IRS tax forms with instructions and other tax information materials faxed to you.

You can order the Federal Tax Forms CD-ROM (Publication 1796) for $25 by calling 1-877-233-6767, or order it for $18 over the Internet at www.irs.ustreas.gov/cdorders. This CD includes current-year and prior-year tax forms with instructions and tax publications.

Dial TeleTax at 1-800-829-4477 twenty-four hours a day, seven days a week, for recorded tax information on approximately 160 tax topics. Automated refund information is available Monday through Friday from 7 A.M. to 11 P.M. and Saturday from 7 A.M. to 4 P.M.

If you use TTY/TDD equipment, call 1-800-829-4059 with your tax questions. You can also order forms and publications through this number.

A "Small Business Corner" has been added to the IRS Web site, making it easier for small-business owners to locate and understand tax information directly related to their needs. There are three major sections: Before Starting Your Business, Operating Your Business, and Employment Taxes. For more information, visit the Web site at www.irs.ustreas.gov/prod/bus_info/sm_bus/index.html.

IRS e-file Program and Payment Options for Small Businesses

The IRS e-file programs offer paperless filing, more convenient filing, faster processing with increased accuracy, and confirmation of filing for small-business owners.

941 TeleFile. This is an e-file option for qualified businesses. It's an inter-active computer program designed to electronically file Form 941, *Employer's Quarterly Federal Tax Return*, using a touch-tone tele-phone. Qualified businesses can call toll-free, follow the voice prompts, and the Telefile system will calculate the tax liability or any overpayment and begin the electronic filing process.

Electronic Federal Tax Payment System (EFTPS). This is the easiest way to make federal tax deposits. It offers you the convenience of mak-ing tax deposits directly by phone or personal computer or through a financial institution. No special equipment is required to use EFTPS, and if you want to use a PC, free Windows-based software is available. For more information and an enrollment form, call EFTPS Customer Service at 1-800-945-8400 or 1-800-555-4477. For TTY/TDD, call 1-800-945-8900.

The IRS Office of Public Liaison and Small Business Affairs

Through a national liaison program, the office maintains daily contact and exchanges information with the IRS's external stakeholders—national organizations representing tax practitioners, payroll processors, volunteer and social services, electronic commerce, state departments of revenue, small-business organizations, and large corporate taxpayers.

Small Businesses with Tax Problems

Individual tax problems should be handled by contacting your local IRS office or the office that mailed you a notice or other correspondence. When IRS employees recognize a problem that has not been resolved through normal channels, they can refer it to the Taxpayer Advocate's Problem Resolution Program (PRP), which has the authority to cut through red tape. Your local taxpayer advocate can offer you special help if you have a significant hardship as a result of a tax problem. For more information, call 1-877-777-4778. For TTY/TDD, call 1-800-829-4059. For more information about the Taxpayer Advocate's PRP, and for a list of PRP addresses, call 1-800-829-3676 and ask for Publication 1546, The Problem Resolution Program of the IRS. You can also visit the Web site at www.irs.ustreas.gov/prod/ind_infor/advocate.html.

Small Business Administration Programs and Services

The Office of Advocacy at the Small Business Administration helps to ensure that Congress and all federal agencies are aware of the needs of small businesses when they propose and consider new laws or regulations. You can contact the Office of Advocacy at (202) 205-6533, or visit the Web site at www.sba.gov/advo.

The SBA Web site offers detailed information on the SBA's and other business services, and links to outside resources on the Web. For more information, go to www.sba.gov.

The SBA has offices throughout the United States. For the nearest one, look under "U.S. Government" in your telephone directory, or call the SBA Answer Desk at 1-800-U-ASK-SBA. The answer desk will address your questions about starting or running a business and how to get assistance. To send a fax to the SBA, call (202) 205-7064.

Index